"Melissa expresses what we all think on a daily basis. Her insight, strength, passion, and sense of sisterhood are a blessing to every law enforcement wife."

"Melissa Littles and The Police Wife Life are a window into the soul of the families behind the Thin Blue Line. Her writing grips the heart and her support of all law enforcement is contagious. You can feel the emotion in every written word and are instantly driven to support the c

Mahoney, Alaska

"Melissa really brings to life the unique struggles and issues that the wives and families of our great police officers go through. Even though her book is targeted towards the wives of the officers, it's a great read for the general public."

"Not only can Melissa make you laugh, and cry, but she helps all LEOWs get through the rough patches in our lives."

L. A. Ward, Texas

"Angels come in many forms. In Melissa we have found a friend, a sister and an inspiration. Her writing expresses the feelings and emotions of all LEO wives."

Kristie W., Raleigh, North Carolina

"Melissa's stories dig deep to the true heart of the matter, the love of a Law Enforcement Wife. She evokes every emotion from laughter to tears with her inspirational words."

Amanda Shoemaker, Missoula, Montana

"Melissa has an amazing ability to pull you through a myriad of emotion in each of her stories. Her writing leaves you wanting more and reminds you that we're not alone."

K. Estrella, Minnesota

The Police Wife Life

Bullets in the Washing Machine

By Melissa Littles

Published by The Police Wife Life

www.thepolicewifelife.com

SUPPORTING LIFE BEHIND THE THIN BLUE LINE

Bullets in the Washing Machine

Melissa Littles

ISBN: 978-0-615-54104-4

The author may be contacted at the following address:
Email: info@thepolicewifelife.com
Web site: www.thepolicewifelife.com

Layout: Tim Priebe, T&S Web Design
Cover photo: Emily Spirek
Cover design: Emily Spirek and Holly Titus,
T&S Web Design
www.tandswebdesign.com

Published in the United States of America

Introduction

As a little girl I remember my mother telling me many things, things that stick with you as you grow. Squinting gives you wrinkles, popping your knuckles is bad, always use real butter when baking. I also remember her teaching me if I were lost, scared or in danger, look for a police officer.

The tides have turned. Somewhere along the way the respect for our law enforcement officers has been lost. They are seen as the enemy. Our officers are being hunted in coffee shops and while sitting in their patrol cars. They are being gunned down in their own precincts. There is a mentality amongst the criminals in our society that the answer to avoiding arrest is to murder an officer.

Our officers are the peacekeepers of our streets and communities. They run into harms way to pull the public to safety. Each time an officer takes his shift he is ready and willing to lay down his life to protect a stranger.

I am the wife of a police officer, although my writings do cater to the wives and families of officers, to lend support to the struggles of this life, to remind those who live in Law Enforcement to remain focused on the big picture, I have another goal as well. To bring awareness back to society, an understanding of the life those in Law Enforcement lead, a reminder that an officer is more than just an enforcer of laws, they are human beings.

Law enforcement officers (LEOs) do not create the laws, they fight the darkness of this world each day with one goal; to serve, protect and make it home alive to those they love.

This book is a compilation of stories, some true to me, some based on the lives of others, but all experiences lived by those in Law Enforcement. I hope that in reading my stories those who live this life will be touched in knowing you are not alone, and although it is not easy at times, we must always remember the big picture.

Bullets In

The Washing Machine

It seemed to always come in waves, the highs and lows in her crazy world. She considered herself a veteran LEO wife, after thirteen years of marriage to this life she felt she had earned her super cape. She would have to consider this week one of the lows, and although she had learned to reserve her raw emotions and to resist the urge to harbor bad thoughts, there were times when she just had to be normal. As she prodded her three children to gather their laundry in the dining room and start separating colors and whites she couldn't help but feel the pang of that forbidden emotion. Indeed, she felt resentment for this life in that moment, although she knew it was just that, a moment.

If you've ever tried to get three children, under the age of ten, to not only separate laundry, but cheerfully and willingly gather their bundles, load up in the SUV in the blazing heat of summer to head out to the closest neighborhood with a laundry mat, then you know, this day would qualify on the low scale of the fun meter. She caught herself before the expletive released from her lips as she jiggled the temperature gauge on the air conditioner. Her worn out SUV was just as much of a sore spot this week as her laundry situation. With all three of her precious cargo venting their disgust at today's events, while barking orders for fast food, the only thing she could focus on was getting to the end of this day. As they arrived at the laundry mat she forced a deep breath and announced to her brood the job at hand.

She looked at his number come across her phone and pondered not answering. She frankly knew herself well enough to know when she was on the brink of an all out explosion of verbal release. However, she had learned from her years in this life, you always put those emotions on hold when he calls, no matter what your personal struggles may be, you push them aside for the sake of the big picture.

"Hey, just checking on you guys," he said it with such a casual tone it almost infuriated her. "Oh, we're fine, I have three children, fighting over washing machines, in an eighty-five degree sauna in a neighborhood which I'm sure you frequent for not so good reasons, and all because you cannot remember to clean out your pockets before you decide to do a load of laundry!" Silence filled the airwaves for a moment while he took in what she had conveyed, while at the same time she absorbed what she had spewed in the heat of the moment. Him, at the same time as her, "I'm sorry," and the laugh they both had shared so many times in the past over circumstances related to this life which took them off the path of anything anyone could compare as normal. "Baby, I love you, I promise we'll get the laundry situation figured out after payday. I'm really sorry, no more bullets in the washing machine," she couldn't really be mad at him, regardless of how hard she tried.

Although this would be the second washing machine to fall victim to his ammo in the last eight years, she knew, this too shall pass. As she began to ask him what he wanted for dinner, she heard the familiar sound which had interrupted her marriage for years. She heard dispatch through the phone and immediately her pulse raced. "Love you, gotta go." And just like that, he was gone.

She stood in her bedroom looking in the mirror at a person she never wanted to know. Although the sedatives her doctor had given her were numbing, she was still very clear about who she saw, and she knew without a doubt, there was no wishing this image away. Her mother and brother stood with her instructing her, leading her, telling her, it was time to go. As they all gathered her children into the family car, she once again put on her cape.

She had learned to wear that cape well over the years, through all the times she had to live this life on her own she had grown accustomed to him not being there. She had planned and attended birthday parties alone. She knew how to represent both of them at parent-teacher conferences. She was a pro at making last minute cancellations with her friends and family. She knew how to convince three little girls that Christmas really always came a day after their friends. But this, she had not accounted for. As much as it made no sense in her head, she still was angry at him. After all she had done on her own, how could he leave her alone to bury him? She kept looking at her family in the car, closing her eyes intermittently hoping against hope he would appear once she opened them. There are just some things that she felt she shouldn't have to handle by herself. She still hadn't resolved herself to doing this at all.

It amazed her how much laundry could pile up when it seemed she had done nothing for days. Her family was finally starting to trickle back to their lives, she was slowly beginning to come out of the haze which had clouded her since the day she got the call. She kept telling herself she needed to get up and bring some order back to their lives. She knew it was time to move past the initial shock of it all, she knew now she would forever have to wear the same cape she always had. She felt as if she were still a police wife, like she always would be, holding down the fort while he was off at battle, keeping their world on a steady keel while they waited to see him once more. It would just be a longer wait now.

She had cried as much as she could, she had held her children as tight as she could hold them. She knew it was time to get on with her life, whatever that may be. She was in her kitchen, clearing through all the food people had brought, reading through cards they had left, amazed at the kindness of others when she heard the doorbell. A moment of irritation swept over her at the interruption in her moment of resolve. Enough kindness already, she told herself not to be rude as she opened the door.

The delivery man stood with his clipboard, completely taken aback by the woman weeping in her doorway. He had no way of knowing the cargo he delivered that day would leave an impression which would last a lifetime. As she signed the delivery slip for her new washer and dryer her husband had purchased for her the day he was killed, she read the special message he included on the delivery instructions.

"I'm sorry, I love you. I promise, no more bullets in the washing machine."

Some Things are Personal

Someone once said to me, "The only reason you're so 'pro-cop' is because you're married to one. Before you married one you never liked to see one coming either, just admit it."

There's actually a little more to it.

She didn't know what had set him off that cold morning in March, all she knew was she had to be at work on time, her employer was quickly growing tired of her excuses and without her job, her escape plan was sure to fail. Of course he was fully aware of that as well. She quickly began going through the routine steps, apologizing, accepting the blame, reassuring him he was right and she was wrong.

She began to nicely and properly beg him to let go of her arm, to please give her car keys back, then she began the bargaining routine. She traded her house key and garage door opener for her car keys knowing as long as she could make it to work on time she could worry about how to get back in the house later. It was all falling into place, his mood seemed to calm as he felt his power growing over her. She began to feel a sense of relief as he dangled her keys in front of her face, until she reached for them.

She knew how to drop to the floor and protect her head with one hand and her torso with the other. She had mastered the tightest fetal position anyone could curl into, yet he always seemed to find the one spot she could not protect. The familiar combination of the sound of silence in the air, the sting of flesh and muscle reacting to the blows, along with the taste of blood in her mouth let her know it was over. She pulled herself up off the bathroom floor, not wanting to look but knowing how much work would need to be done to cover it, she looked at the clock instead. 8:22 a.m. Twenty-two minutes late for work. She looked around the bathroom floor. No keys. She went to the window and looked out to the driveway, he was gone. She went to her purse, no phone, no wallet, no keys. The normalcy of the routine being completed, just as it always was. She returned to the bathroom to begin to fix things, again.

They say everyone has their breaking point, the moment of truth, the point of no return. As she looked in the bathroom mirror she saw someone looking back at her she did not recognize. She could feel an unusual sense of clarity and anger and resolve beginning to rise to the surface, she could sense something she had not felt in over a year. The longer she stared at the reflection, the more her blood began to boil.

She no longer heard the voice telling her to, "stick with the plan, the plan will work, just a few more months, it will work", instead she began to feel an overwhelming sense of urgency to ignore the stranger staring back at her and to pay attention to herself. For whatever reason, in that very moment, she had finally come back and she never questioned again, it was time. She didn't even notice the look or surprise or horror on her neighbors face when the door opened and she asked to borrow the phone.

She should have known them by name, those officers who always seemed to be the ones who came to her rescue. For all the times they had responded to the neighbors calls that brought them to her house, she always apologized profusely, her level of embarrassment and humiliation always being at the forefront of her mind. She knew what they must think of her, they knew she worked in Law, but look at the dysfunction which was her behind closed doors reality. She knew she was nothing but a fool to them, an unwanted interruption in their day. Just another story to laugh about - that stupid woman who stays with that monster. She pictured them leaving each time making bets at how quickly they would be back again. Today, she would begin to learn the truth about more than just herself.

As she stood in her neighbors doorway, she heard the voice on the other end of the phone asking her to stay on the line, reassuring her they were on their way, then she saw his car come around the corner and pull back into the driveway. His eyes were locked on her and she recognized that look very well. She began to feel the whole world moving in some form of slow motion as he emerged from the car. This was the moment she knew would come and she said only two more words to the voice on the phone, "Please, hurry."

In the months that followed she began to have a newfound respect for those men who came to her rescue, time and time again. Those men she always thought viewed her as a nuisance and a joke. That day she found herself running from her neighbors porch and subsequently fighting for her life those men saved her, once again. They had been called so many times before, she really didn't think they would rush over so quickly, but they did.

They rushed into a line of fire and fought a 6'2", 240 lb monster high on rage and fury who was on an unstoppable mission to serve justice of his own. And they surprised her after that, in many little ways. They told her they had been keeping an eye on him for months. They watched him from a distance, never on a mission, just on alert. They explained how that was normal for them, knowing their community, being aware of those who have brought attention to themselves. She never considered any of that before now. She was also made aware that she would not be forgotten in the long months she had ahead of her waiting for the monster to go to trial, they never spoke those words to her, it was actions.

Here and there, things she never noticed before, like the glimpse of a patrol car at the end of her block when she arrived home from work, or one of the many nights she still couldn't sleep, looking out the window and seeing the tail lights of a cruiser who just happened to be driving by at 3:00 a.m., or how that one officer started sitting in the church parking lot across the street from her neighborhood to do his paperwork at the end of his shift. She knew she was nothing special, there was no organized mission to help her, she soon realized that was the point. She didn't have to be special to them, it was their job to be there for her, and they were.

As the days on the calendar began to pass, she grew more anxious. As much as she prided herself on escaping him, she had not escaped the damage that had been done. It had been a year since then and yet still some nights she slept sitting up, gun in hand, waiting for him to fulfill his promise to return and finish the job. She became almost compulsive about looking out her windows, every sound creating a brief moment of panic within her. She would see the District Attorney's number on her phone and instantly become nauseous at the thought of reliving it. She knew the day was coming and she knew if she ever truly wanted it to be over she would have to face him, she would have to stand up to him and as much as she was terrified on the inside she knew she would have to let him know she would never fear him again.

She had walked the halls of the courthouse thousands of times before. She was the calmer of fears, the voice of reason, the one who ensured her clients that today would be a good day, a turning point in their lives, the start of something new. She never anticipated finding herself shaken with fear on her own familiar turf that morning, but that is exactly how she felt. The clatter of dress shoes coming down the marble halls had her dreading the inevitable, which set of shoes would be his? She kept her head down, pretending to read her notes, waiting for the courtroom to open, praying it did before he arrived.

Her eyes wandered over to the shoes already in her view - they were nice shoes. Oddly her mind drifted a bit and she found herself slightly giggling to herself for just a moment at how perfectly shiny and clean and un-scuffed those shoes were. She found it entertaining as now she understood exactly why they were shoes in perfect condition; they belong to that officer who stood there beside her. She had learned in the past few months that those officers can be very particular about certain things. She didn't want to distract him from his duty but she couldn't help herself, "Nice shoes," she said. He just gave her a look, then continued looking straight ahead down the hall, on his mission of protecting her as she waited. As she entered the courtroom with her attorney she could feel his presence in the back of the room. As the monster made his entrance, she couldn't help but wish the man with the nice shoes would come stand right in front of her.

The time had come. She had waited a year for this, she had endured the nightmare of her life for another year prior to it. She had done everything in her power to stay strong, despite the stalking and harassing and internet bashing and threats and violations of the protective orders time and time again. She knew the law, she had over twenty years of experience behind her, much of which she still struggled to rely on, after all, look how wrong she had been on this issue.

Within seconds of her taking the witness stand she felt every possible emotion begin to overcome her. Fear, shame, humiliation, sheer terror. Her focus was shifting, she felt herself becoming lost in her thoughts. She was doing what she trained her witnesses to never do - panic. She had to composed herself, she did not come all this way to let him do this to her again, she knew this was her moment to take back her life but she felt herself completely falling apart. Then, she heard those shoes.

Those shoes began walking up to the first row of seats in the courtroom followed by the slight sound of metal contacting wood as his gun brushed against the arm of the chair as he sat down. The monster bolstered his objection of having an officer in the courtroom, he objected to being harassed and intimidated with such an unnecessary show of force. After asking repeatedly for the officer to be removed, the monster was matter of factly informed by the presiding Judge; "This man is an officer of this court, it is his duty to provide protection and support to those in need, and I believe this woman is in need of both, and he will not be removed from my courtroom, and you will show him the respect he deserves."

As she looked over at the man with the shoes, she felt she should acknowledge him, the Judge's words powerful and still lingering in the air. The officer was already looking back, his eyes locked on hers with a sense of purpose. He gave her that same look he had in the hall, the look of being seriously concentrated on his mission of protection. He then silently mouthed three words, "I love you."

That was the moment I knew without a doubt, Officer Littles would be on a mission to protect me for the rest of my life. And it was a good day, and a new start, and a new life after all.

So you see, I am grateful for our officers.

If you know someone in an abusive relationship or you are being abused, there is help. One in every three women are victims of domestic violence in their lifetime. There are resources available for those in need. Call the domestic violence hotline at 1-800-799-SAFE for help.

The Big Picture

It was just a typical day, kids playing, house cleaning, dealing with all the errands. Soccer practice on one field and softball on another, at the same time. She almost laughed out loud at the sound of her own mother's voice coming out of her mouth as she announced, "I don't know how many times I have to tell you to make sure you have your cleats! Am I talking just to hear myself talk?" She had to laugh, so she wouldn't cry. Once again, she left one daughter at one field, asked a parent to keep an eye out for her, loaded back up to dash home, to dig through a pile of clothes on her other daughter's floor. What does it take to just put the clothes in the hamper, a wet towel, are you joking? Completely frazzled she found the somewhat damp and now very smelly cleats and headed back to the first field. She delivered the shoes along with, "the look", and began watching the clock. Thirty minutes. That's how much time she would spend at each game. Long enough to just miss the best play either of them would make. It never failed. As soon as she drove away a parent would text her, "Goal!" or "Double!" She had no time to dwell; she was off and running again over to the ball park. Thirty minutes. And so it went 3 nights a week for practice and games, by herself.

She did not complain, it's not as if any of this could be helped. She looked at the bleachers and caught herself looking at the couples, sets of parents, together at the same time. She quickly found the single parents to focus on; see, she wasn't the only one. Just then her cell phone rang. "Emily had a little fall, you need to get back over here as soon as you can."

She did her best to block out her other daughter during the hurried car ride back to the other complex. Now was not the time for a million questions, coupled with complaints of being, "pulled from the best game ever." She was doing her best to drive while trying to reach her husband. She called twice, it rang, it didn't go straight to voicemail, which was a good sign, probably just a traffic stop and he'll call right back. She texted him some form of a horribly spelled message. She refused to worry about proper grammar while driving, especially with Chatty Cathy in the back seat reminding her so smartly that texting while driving kills people, "just like Dad says." That was her breaking point, she had reached her limit.

The words flew out of her mouth with such fury she even took herself aback. "JUST LIKE DAD SAYS?! WELL WHERE IS MR. SUPERHERO NOW?! IF YOUR DAD WERE HERE I WOULDN'T HAVE TO TEXT WHILE DRIVING NOW WOULD I? BUT HE'S NOT HERE! HE'S NEVER HERE, SO HUSH YOUR MOUTH!"

As she sat in the emergency room, waiting with Chatty Cathy, who was now reduced to Maligned Molly, her guilt started taking over. "I'm sorry, I shouldn't have said that, I was just really frustrated and I didn't mean that." Her 11 year old looked up at her so matter-of-fact, without hesitation and said "Yes you did, it's the truth." She held back the tears and quietly told her to stay put while she once again headed outside to try and get a signal so she could reach her husband. Three hours later, she loaded her cranky, tired, hungry girls into the SUV and headed to the fast food drive thru, then to the 24 hour pharmacy to get the prescription filled, ice packs, ace bandages and all the other things on the list for a bad sprain. She didn't even know why she bothered to check her phone for a missed call.

Six long hours after she left the house for two games, she finally arrived home, unloaded her girls and their gear, fast food bags, drinks, crutches, prescriptions and her purse. With her hands completely full, trying to get an injured teen into the house, NOW her phone finally decides to ring?

Exasperated, exhausted, frazzled and frankly angry at this point, while leaving a trail of falling items all throughout the garage, she managed to answer the call. The voice on the other end gruffly stated, "What took you so long to answer?" Tears rolling down her face she took a deep breath and calmly stated, "I've got my hands full here, how are you?" Time stood still as she heard the words while trying to make them register in her mind. He spoke in a flurry of quick yet pointed information, "Joe's been shot, I'm fine but I've got to keep looking for the bastard who did this. I tried to call you before you saw the news but I couldn't get to my phone. I saw where you've called, I know you've probably been scared sick babe, I'm sorry. I love you and I'm safe, know that. I can't talk right now, I've got to do this for Joe. I'm sorry Baby, I'll be home safe as soon as I can, I promise you."

All she managed to get out before he hung up was "I love you, be careful."

Before she could even try to compose herself she looked up to the glares of her children and she knew that they knew. It's a known form of communication without speaking, she could hide it when they were little, but they were old enough to read her now. She could sense their panic and realized the look on her own face was the cause of it. "Daddy is fine girls, he's just fine." Her oldest held up her phone, showed her mother the text from her best friend, "They shot my Dad!" How in the world was she going to handle this one...alone.

All three of them, in one bed, watching movies to pass the time, her oldest a little calmer now that she knew her friend's father and her husband's partner of

10 years would live, the surgery was successful, he was so lucky this time. Still, the thought of being in separate rooms was not even an option. She kept her girls close, kept making trips back to the kitchen, swapping out ice packs, waiting for time to pass. It was almost 5:00 a.m. before all three of them sat straight up in her bed; the garage door and a sigh of relief heard round the world.

They held each other, no words spoken but everything being said. She thanked God over and over in her mind as she pressed her cheek against his neck. He kissed her, looked past her to their bedroom to his daughters and a pile of pillows and towels and ice. "Oh my God what happened? Is she alright? Are you alright?" She quickly and calmly reassured him, "It's just a little sprain, no big deal, I promise she's fine, really. Go take a shower and I'll get them to bed."

As the familiar feeling of family failure began to wash over him, once again being totally oblivious to his own family's needs, the magnitude of everything that had happened that day began to rise up in a fury, which was quickly quieted by the steady voice of his wife. As always, she knew just how to handle him, how to calm him, how to make him let go, if just long enough to rest.   "Hurry up and shower, your food's getting cold."

Always remember the big picture.

An Officer's Worth

As I update this, it is April 19, 2011. In the past 24 hours, we have lost two officers and another K-9. In the past week, we have lost three officers and two K-9's. As of the week of April 5, 2011, when I originally wrote this, we had lost two police officers to gunfire in a 72 hour period, both fatally shot in the face, another critically injured, and a K-9 stabbed to death. Just over four weeks ago seven officers were gunned down in seven days. To date, we are only four months into 2011 and we have lost sixty officers in the line of duty. Not only have we lost them to gunfire, we have lost them to strangulation, stabbings and even had one pushed to his death. An officer is dying every other day in America, yet there is no movement to stop this madness.

You can never begin a plea for awareness involving law enforcement officers without immediately being confronted with those who have no regard for our officers. There will always be the masses who have no respect for our officers, what they do to protect our streets and communities, or where society would be without them. There is no disputing that there are corrupt officers in this country, those with no respect for their badge, those who abuse their power for evil purposes. I have stated many times before, those who abuse the badge and do not live up to its honor should be dealt with just as the criminals they are.

However, statistics prove those officers are minuscule in number compared to the mass majority of honorable officers who have dedicated their lives to protecting and serving their communities regardless of the hatred they face from the public, regardless of the dangers they are subjected to each and every shift. You will never sway those who have made the decision to hate our peace keepers. They have formulated their reasons and regardless of the factual statistics or proof of positive actions by our officers, those who hate them will always hate them as a whole, based on the actions of those few who are corrupt.

But most of those who hate our officers are not the same people who are murdering our officers. Most of those that hate our officers are simply those who's lives are disrupted by the expectation of being a law abiding citizen of the country which allows them their freedom to begin with. Those that hate our police officers on American soil are the same who will stand up and support our American troops abroad, for our troops do not impact their illegal lifestyle at home. Those who hate our officers at home would be the same who would turn on our troops the second they began to police our streets in America, as the impact would affect their illegal lifestyle.

Frankly, those who hate the police officers of America would hate anyone who tried to police their illegal lifestyle, so in all honestly, those who hate our police officers in essence will really never matter. It is those who are honest, law abiding citizens of this country who need to be made aware of the price being paid as our officers are being murdered at the rate of one every 42 hours.

There is no doubt that there is a sense of complacency across this country at the death of our police officers. Those who hate them rejoice temporarily and get back to work breaking the law. Average citizens look up at the news briefly, feel sorrow momentarily and express the commonality which needs to change, that the death of an officer is merely part of the job. A risk which every officer knowingly, willingly and expectedly signs up for when he takes the badge. The truth is, our officers did not sign up for what is taking their lives at the rate of one officer every 42 hours.

An officer signs up for a call to duty. A call that is part of who they are as human beings. They sign up to knowingly, willingly and eagerly to protect and serve their communities, night and day, regardless of circumstance or weather or holidays. They sign up to protect every stranger who needs their help. They sign up, willing to run full speed into harms way in order to protect those strangers. They run towards bullet fire, they stand in the face of unknown dangers. As they respond to auto accidents they will risk being run over themselves. As they respond to domestic calls they will face hostile couples aggravated with adrenaline who turn their aggression onto them. As they respond to hostage situations they will spend hours, sometimes days in the elements forced to remain collected, focused, ready for chaos at a moments notice, while hungry and on little sleep, much less with a bathroom. They will respond to murder scenes involving innocent children, they will learn to handle the smell of charred skin, rotten flesh, maggots and human waste. They will encounter decomposed bodies of children who are the same ages of their own. They will find women bound, gagged, raped, murdered who look just like their wives.

They will plead with prostitutes to allow them to help them so they don't have to recover their body in the weeks to come. They will be called out to gang infested territory to drive by shootings where mothers lose their children on a daily basis, yet they will be hated upon their arrival. They will be spit on, threatened, targeted by many for their dedication to do their duty despite their circumstance. They will be vomited on, stabbed with dirty needles, punched, kicked, urinated on and worse. They will wrestle drunks and drug addicts and remove scared, abused children from their homes and have no choice but to leave them with strangers of the State. And they signed up for that. The knowingly, willingly, eagerly signed up for that. What is that worth?

An officer does more than just that which he signed up for. Every single shift he walks away from his family, not ever knowing if today is the day he will never return. He signed up for that. He and his family knowingly, willingly signed up for the risk of the loss of his life, and they accept that risk, and they live with the fear and anxiety each and every day that today may be the day his maker calls. An officer must live each day knowing he has no choice but to put the needs of complete strangers ahead of his own wife and children and family members. He signed up for that and he accepts it. What is that worth?

An officer lives each day with shift hours that constantly change, calls that come at the end of his shift which leave him working hours after he was already exhausted. He works hungry and sleep deprived. He will go days crossing paths with his family, arriving home while they sleep or have already left for the next day. He will not see his children awake most days and when he does, he will rarely have more than a moment to enjoy them.

An officer lives each day knowing his wife has not had his attention or time or household help for weeks on end, and as much as he wants to be there an officer knows his wife has learned to live life as if she were single. An officer lives life in a way feeling like an outsider at times in a life he is rarely present for. He will come home with the horrific images and memories in his head, yet he will not inflict or impose those on his wife as he already feels guilty for what she endures, and certainly does not want her living with what he lives with. He signed up for that. He knowingly, willingly accepts that as part of his duty. What is that worth?

In today's society our officers who have signed up for so much of their own will are being subjected to so much more, and it is not just a risk, it is not just part of the job, it is not something that should be expected of them. They are being subjected to the blatant disregard for their lives. They are being subjected to a society with such a poor perception of an officer's worth that when an officer falls, it goes unnoticed. And they are not falling due to the everyday risks they signed up for. They are being murdered. They are being assassinated. They are being sought out, singled out, targeted purposely by repeat, convicted felons who are being released back on to the streets of America time and time again. Repeat convicted felons with nothing to lose and no regard for human life who have learned by experience there is no long term consequence for assaulting a police officer.

There are no laws in this country to give anyone any reason to respect an officer. They are the protectors of our streets and communities, they are the only ones who have that job, they are the only ones we rely on to perform those duties yet our states and government do not see fit to deter anyone from taking them for granted. There is every level of expectation that our officers should perform every single duty they might encounter, regardless of circumstance, no matter what the danger, and yet in return there is no respect or regard for what they do, and more so than not, there is no value placed on our officer's lives.

There must be an awakening in America as a whole, within its communities and cities and local, state and national government. America needs to be awakened as to the value of our officers and their worth. Their worth not only as the officer's we rely on and hold to a level of expectation to perform those duties they knowingly, willingly and eagerly signed up for, but their worth as human beings. Human beings who make the daily sacrifices expected of them, sacrifices only they make as no one else will. Human beings who have knowingly, willing, eagerly signed up to make the ultimate sacrifice for each and every one of us, every single day, every single shift.

There needs to be an awakening that our officers deserve protection from their society and their government. They deserve to be held to a higher level of protection. They should be revered, just as our troops are. Our government is swift and with a mighty hand when someone comes after our troops. Why not our officers? Our government, with conviction, will immediately and permanently remove anyone from society who injures or murders a member of Congress, a governor, any politician really. Why not our officers? America needs to be awakened and ask themselves the question, where would we be without our police officers? What is an officer's worth? To me, my officer is worth the world.

Please, support our Law Enforcement Officers.

No Regrets,

Just Lessons Learned

The morning light began trickling in through the drapes, making the dust in the air float in a dance around the room. The silence was deafening, although he was still unable to shake the sound of her cries from his mind. He knew the sunlight meant the time was near. Soon, he would have to pick himself up off the couch and tend to the task at hand. As he sat up, he felt the effects of his age wash over his entire body. Every muscle ached, a combination of tenseness and the lack of a soft bed. The pit in his stomach had still not subsided. As he tried to stretch his body into some relief the thought of what today would bring began to slowly unravel in his mind. Should he make her something to eat? Brew some coffee? The kitchen was bursting with food that had been delivered from every source known to mankind, although in the three days that had passed, he had yet to see her touch so much as a glass of water. He kept bringing himself back to that light coming through the window. He had learned over the years how to judge the time of day based merely on shadows and angles and the placement of the sun. As he forced himself off the couch, he began the long walk up the stairs.

She was sitting in the window seat, her eyes fixated on the house just a few doors down the street. He could hear the sounds of children's voices and he instantly knew it was the two little boys from across the street. Many times he had wanted to burst out of bed and bang on the window, or march over there and instill some discipline and manners which were clearly lacking. Obviously, their own mother had just as little regard for an entire cul-de-sac being awakened each Saturday morning at 8:00 a.m. sharp by the shrieks and shrills of those two running amuck up and down the street. She always stopped him though. His frustration at her lack of understanding that he rarely, if ever, was afforded a Saturday morning in bed. Now that he had semi-retired, he thought he deserved at least that much. Today was the last day she needed to hear all that racket. He began to turn back to the stairway when he heard her speak. It was the first words she had spoken since literally crying her voice into silence two days prior. She said what she had said every Saturday morning at the sounds of the children's voices, "No, let them play."

He gingerly approached her, as gingerly as a man of his making could. For the first time he was completely lost. He had no idea what to say or do or how to help her. He was always able to fix it. Always. Perhaps not to her liking, but he always found a solution to any situation, and the matter at hand was resolved. This, he could not fix, and he was fully aware that she felt it too. As he stood beside her he noticed something in her hands. He hadn't seen it in years, hardly even remembered it until he saw it. The little metal police car. He had stopped to pick up some beer on the way home one day, many years ago, seemed like a lifetime ago now, and right there at the checkout he had seen them in the package. He was never one for spoiling, he had enough of that nonsense to deal with from their mother, but these were cheap enough and there were no reports of mischief out of them this week. He grabbed two of the little cars and placed them on the counter. When he arrived home that evening she was just placing the dinner plates on the table. He put the little cars on the counter and proceeded to open his first beer.

They came running into the kitchen, their shrills and squeals echoing down the hall. Just 14 months apart, what once was an overwhelming task for her, two babies so close together, had been replaced by two boys, inseparable and each other's best friend. Her eyes widened as she gave them, "the look" as they came barreling into the kitchen, as if to say, "Settle down, your father is home," without ever speaking it at all. Normally, "the look" would have sufficed, but they had both seen the little toy cars on the counter and there was no stopping them now. She waited for his command, she knew he would not bend the rules. He always believed in being strict: a time for work, a time for play, a time to eat, a time to speak. That is how you raise boys into responsible men. But the command never came.

Instead, she found herself watching what seemed to be a scene from someone else's life, one of the neighbor's lives perhaps, where the children could run and sing and dance and play as loud as they could, even in the front yard where all could see and hear them. No, that was nothing like her life with her children. Her life was about keeping them quiet while he slept, keeping them in the backyard to play, not out in the open. Being very selective of who was allowed to come over, and never did she allow them out of her sight. It's just the way it was. And that is why that moment, that out of place, out of character moment, made such an impression and memory that day.

She would never forget him laying on the floor with her two boys, racing the little metal police cars up and down his legs, over his belly, across the floor again and again. Their smiles and giggles and pure joy in that moment, and how ever since that day, they wanted to be just like their father. And he would never realize the importance of that day until another day, a day many years later, when the memory of the little metal police car would come back to him as she held it in her hands. Now, in that moment, her sitting in the window seat, running her fingers over the little metal car, it's paint chipped and worn, it's years of play showing, he reached out, wiped the tear from her cheek and gently said, "I am so very sorry."

He never thought he could feel anguish. True, unfiltered, gut wrenching anguish. Three days before it just hadn't sunk in, and three days before he was the one who had to maintain his strength in order to hold her up. It wasn't until today that he began to fully accept the reality, the truth that could never be changed. He found himself wishing for memories he could not produce, time he could not get back. His regrets started to flow through his mind. He could not remember things most fathers should know. When did he teach him to ride a bike? Why couldn't he remember that? Why didn't they ever go fishing? He kept trying to stop himself, to focus on the task at hand, but his mind was relentlessly trying to recount something, anything, and he could only grasp on to one day. That day he laid down on the floor and played with his sons with those little metal police cars.

It was at that very moment the most gut wrenching realization came to mind. If he could only remember that one day; that one time he was home when they were awake, that one time he didn't let the stress of his day dictate the rest of theirs, that one moment when he allowed himself to just be a dad and for them to just be little boys playing with their Daddy, what if that was the only memory his sons had of him?

As he looked around the church, a sea of blue engulfed the room. Standing room only and countless other officers outside the doors. Of course he expected nothing less considering the circumstance, after all, he was the Chief, and the officer down was his firstborn son.

As he looked to his left he saw his wife of thirty years, one hand clutching the little police car, the other clutching onto the arm of her only living child, his dress uniform crisp and perfectly worn, his shoes without a mark, his badge gleaming, his heart breaking. He looked across his wife into the eyes of the little boy he played with on the floor that day so many years ago and he saw the pain in his eyes, the loss of his only brother, his best friend. He felt like an outsider in a way. Just by looking at them holding on to each other, somehow keeping each other going, he began to realize how much his tough skin and tall walls and barrier against emotion had cost him. He kept looking at the little metal car in his wife's hand and he began to hate the life it seemed to have created.

After all was said and done, they made the long drive back home. Exhausted, mentally spent and emotionally empty, he knew he had to maintain for a few more hours. Family would come, friends would be there soon to offer their condolences and bring more food and flowers and prayers. He didn't know how much more he could take without breaking, but he was trained to be strong in times like these. His wife could sense him beginning to falter. She had her own regrets: not reaching out to him, not knowing how to comfort him. She had spent a lifetime allowing him to handle the bad times in his own way, and now she had no idea what he needed from her. She was so lost in her own grief the past three days she really didn't recall much of anything. Maybe it was because it was over now, maybe because she had made it through the funeral, but for the first time she began to see him, her husband, not the Chief, and the pain he wore.

She took his hand, looked him in the eyes and said to him, "Don't ever regret who you are. If you weren't the officer you were you would have been dead years ago, and our children would never have had a father. They grew into strong men because of you, they realize how to take care of others first because of you, they were raised seeing me live life without you but always knowing it was because you were out there, protecting the world and keeping our home a safe place to live. They became officers because they idolized you and they saw the men they wanted to be and they became that because of you."

She grabbed his hand and placed the little metal police car in it and said, "The day you laid on the floor with him and played with this little car was the day he connected with you as a father. He knew you were not just a police officer. He saw you as his Daddy who was a police officer, and ever since that day both of those boys knew they wanted to grow up just like you. Our son gave his life with character which was born from you. He never backed down, he fought until the end and he died honoring his badge. He would never, ever have wanted any other life than what he had. He died with more integrity and strength than most men ever possess, and he learned that from you."

He began to sob; years of emotion he had never let escape, years of regrets and all the fears he had earlier that day, that his son died not knowing him as a father, that he died without memories worthy of taking to the grave. He could no longer maintain his role as the Chief that day. He wept as she held him, this time her strength holding him up, and once again they knew they would make it another day, somehow, they would go on.

As he began to compose himself he heard the sound of his grandsons coming down the hall. Not old enough to fully understand the totality of the day, just as little boys do, their laughter and giggles echoed as they neared. Knowing his state of mind she quickly gave them, "the look" as if to say, "Not now boys, your Grampy has had enough today." She began to turn and lift her finger to quiet them; he took her hand and kissed it. He handed his oldest grandson the little metal police car, looked his wife in the eyes and said...

"No, let them play."

Are You Ready?

You will hear it for the rest of your married life, "You signed up for this." And you did. But did you know? Did you have a clue? Do you now? Do you get it? Do you really get what it means to live the life you have chosen? Because now more than ever, the rules have changed. Even those who signed up years ago are having to adjust to a whole new set of rules. There is a whole new level of evil which has been added to the mix. Each day it seems the disrespect for this life you have chosen rises, are you ready to deal with all that comes with this life?

Are you ready to let him walk out the door into the face of evil and not come home to you? Are you ready to deal with the phone call that he has been hurt or worse in the middle of the night? Are you ready? You better get ready. You better reach down deep inside you and grab your big girl panties and get a plan in place. Have you seen the numbers, I know you have. Have you made sense of them in your head? Have you paid attention to the increase in the last three years? Are you ready if you are the next family to have to go through it? Are you ready? I hope so.

Are you ready for the long hours, the days spent away from each other? Are you prepared for the sleepless nights and the endless days? Are you ready to spend the nights he is home holding him as he relives his battles while his body sleeps out of sheer exhaustion but his mind wrestles demons in the dark? Are you ready to face your own battles alone while waiting for his shoulder to cry on, his touch, his attention, his intimacy, only to be denied due to a drunk driver or a prostitute or a couple who hates each other and depend on him to solve their problems? Are you ready to give up your rare time with your husband because regardless of how good you look or smell or dress or how seductive you are you cannot compete with those who claimed his energy long before he finally made it home? Are you ready to cry in your sleep silently as he will never notice anyway? Can you do it? Can you do it with love? Can you do it without resentment? Can you do it and remain faithful?

Can you pick up his uniform covered in the blood of a child just like yours and clean it for him? Can you look in his eyes and see the pain and suffering and accept that he cannot tell you about it? Can you pick him up at the hospital, take him home and send him back out the next day? Do you have it in you to give up your friends and family for his job? Are you ready to have him disrespected constantly and keep your mouth shut? Can you lead by example and continually present a positive image for the sake of the badge only to be consistently disparaged by those you have never met and who have no right to judge you? Even more so, are you ready for the same treatment from your own family?

Are you ready to spend every minute of every day with the thought of losing him in the back of your mind? Can you accept that he will always put the needs of strangers before your own? Can you deal with planning your anniversary dinner only to have him not be there and not hate him for it? Are you prepared to explain to your children why he didn't show up for their birthday party even though he just called and said he was right around the corner? Are you ready for sporting events alone? Are you ready for parents to ask you how long you have been divorced because they have never seen your husband? Are you ready for their judgment when you explain why he has never been seen?

Can you deal with those who constantly want a piece of him? Are you ready to trust him completely when you cannot contact him for hours at a time even after his shift has ended? Are you ready for him to be in constant contact with dispatchers who are single and partners who have so much in common with him? Can you handle it? Are you ready for accusations of infidelity, corruption and wrong doing and still support and love him? Do you have a clear understanding of how quickly you will destroy it by constantly questioning him and allowing your insecurities to get the best of you? Are you ready for this relationship to be mostly about him and rarely if ever about you? Are you ready for the "we" that this life creates and can you be not only satisfied with it, but fulfilled by it and not resentful of it? Can you see past it to the big picture?

Are you ready to defend this life? Are you ready to embrace it? Are you ready to embrace him and his profession and all this calling represents? Can you send him out to others when you need him for yourself? Do you get it? Loving a police officer is not like loving any other person, it is hard, it is painful and it is rewarding. You have to be ready and you have to get it. Do you understand what you signed up for?

It is not about you and him. It is about his life. His calling will always come first to him, other people will always be his priority even on his days off. If he is called he will go. He does not have a job. He was called to do this and it is who he is and what he is. It is more than a job to him. It is a way of life. He will always be a police officer to others before he is a husband to you. Are you ready? Can you handle it?

I hope you understand and I hope you have a plan in place to assist you if something bad happens to him. You have to have a support system in place for the everyday world which pulls him from you, you must also have support for the unthinkable. You cannot live this life with your head in the sand thinking it won't happen to you or him. You have to be prepared for it. You cannot dwell on it for if you do it will ruin you. You have to learn to put the worry and fear in the back of your mind and not dwell upon it. If you allow it to take over it will drive you away from him and it will destroy what you have with him. You cannot control the fear, you have to learn to accept it and live despite it or it will destroy you. Learn to make the most out of what time you have with him and cherish each and every moment like it is the last moment, and you will make it. Trust him, trust his training and trust his will to live. Support him, love him even when you want to hate him, forgive him.

Develop a safe haven in your home for him. Never allow him out of your site angry. Make it your goal to have him fighting for another chance to make it home to you. Never send him off feeling as if the evil of the streets is a reprieve from the turmoil of his home. Understand that you have a place in his heart but his life is occupied by others, others that need him, others that haunt him, others that beckon him. Listen to him when he can talk about it and hold him in the darkness when he can't talk about it. Allow him time to transition from work to home, there is no off switch, it can't be turned off when he parks the car in the driveway. Ask for help when you feel overwhelmed. Seek guidance from those of us who have more experience in this life and pray.

This life we live is full of every emotion you could possibly encounter, it is never dependable, it is always stressful, it is rarely compassionate to your needs, but if you can do it, if you can embrace it, if you can learn to accept it and all that comes with it, it can be the most rewarding life you ever imagined. It can bring you a respect and closeness and depth of love for your husband rarely experienced in most relationships these days. It is a walk of faith and trust and respect and endurance and perseverance. It takes hard work. It takes dedication. It takes commitment. All marriages take that; but a LEO marriage takes one thing more. It takes knowing your husband could be the next officer down. And it takes you saying, "Yes. I signed up for that."

Pray every single day. Believe in God and trust His plan for you.

Thoughts of a Sleep Deprived

LEO Wife

Most times, I envy the sleepers. Those who can find a way to shut their minds off long enough to recoup and reenergize. I guess I should be happy I have always run effectively enough on low fuel, so to speak, but there are times I wish I could sleep through all this that continually spins around in my head.

However, there are other times, times like now, in the early morning hours before the rest of the world has started moving about that I sit and enjoy being awake to soak it all in, take notes in memories of it all. I sit here in my living room, knowing my children are fast asleep in their warm beds in their cool rooms with their full stomachs. I know they will awaken without fear of being beaten or going hungry, I know they will wake up happy, maybe even grumpy because they are so blessed that they have no idea how happy they should actually be.

As I sit here in my peaceful place I listen to the sounds of a very tired man, sleeping through exhaustion and wrestling the demons he will awaken to face once again so his children can continue to wake up with nothing but peace and happiness and the security which is so readily available to them. I sit here and I try to imagine the burden he bears. The fear he denies, the unspeakable knowledge that even in a place thought to be safer than most, he still listens to the realities literally dying all around his world. I know he reflects on the countless times he has approached a suspect who was just sitting in a car. I know he knows exactly how many doors he has kicked in not knowing what was on the other side. I know he knows he is not faster than the bullet these bastards have learned to aim everywhere his vest does not cover. I know he knows his vest is no match for the ammo they choose to use as a guarantee to win against a warrant.

I sit here and I wonder what must go through his mind every second that he is out there now. I wonder when he started to feel the change. I wonder if his mind wanders to the places mine does when I think of him pulling over an SUV with a soccer mom sticker on the back only to wonder now....will this be the one? Because now, you cannot know if this will be the one.

I wrestle with the conflict of wondering has the change made them better? Has the evil rising awakened them to the need to be hyper vigilant, overly cautious and continually suspicious? Have they really always been that "on" or has it changed for them? I struggle with the thought of it knowing that to ponder such a thing is in essence to say.....did they all have to die to wake them up? Is this what it takes? And I think I have to entertain that because society believes that.

It is the way humans operate, a mentality that it takes a disaster to revive the human spirit. I do not choose to believe that way. I choose to think it is not because of the numbers rising they have had no choice but to awaken to a whole new level of alertness, but rather that they have become awakened to a whole new level of evilness which has always existed, but just as the world continues in the demise of its morals, so does evil increase in its perception of power over goodness. And for as much reason as I have to be a cynic, I still cannot allow myself to stop being an optimist. I cannot go there because I sit here, in my peace, while my children are dreaming the good dreams and while my husband still breathes. He doesn't just have life left in him, but a spark. Not just a spark of life, but a fire and a passion for this thing he does, day in, day out. This "protecting and serving", which is still, despite the numbers, despite the evil, despite the lack of existence of personal peace for him, this thing he still does with conviction. That is proof of good over evil.

So as I sit here in my little bit of peace on earth, I know he will awaken shortly and armor himself like a warrior once again. He will head outside this little place of peace on earth and he will once again do his part. He will stand his position in the thin blue line and he will not let the evil take him without a fight. I believe he lives to fight this battle, to prove to evil it has no place here, it is not wanted and it will not be freely given a ticket to this show called life.

And to think that anyone would not consider him a hero is to me proof that evil is not winning this battle, for if it were, goodness would be desperate for a hero.

Though they may fall while fighting the war, the battle is far, far from over.

Blessed are the peacemakers, for they shall be called the sons of God. (Matthew 5:9)

Gods Plan

She felt as if she was hovering over her own body, looking in from the outside, a spectator gazing through a fog or a haze of confusion. Nothing made any sense, it was all too much to bear. She looked down the hospital corridor and all she could think was, "Please Lord, just let me wake up, this cannot be real."

The halls were bulging with an ocean of blue, lining the walls like water pressed against the floodgates. She watched them as they looked through the double doors, then back to her again. They reminded her of him, constantly checking their watches, fidgeting with their wedding bands, their ears periodically leaning in unison toward the voice inside the radio on their shoulders. They were like synchronized swimmers and she found herself focused on them, watching their dance, only tonight, their dance was off. They were out of sync, unable to help, unable to protect, unable to save one of their own, and they were forced to do as she was, they were forced to wait.

She found it maddening, almost unbearable that each white coat or green set of scrubs coming through those doors were not bringing any news. She didn't know how many times she could repeat herself tonight. "Thank you for coming, we don't know anything yet, he's in surgery, that's all we know." Although she appreciated the support she could not get past the gut wrenching nausea which had enveloped her and only grown stronger with each minute that passed. It had only been four hours since it all began yet it seemed like an eternity.

It was a bad call from the beginning, a domestic involving a couple her husband had dealt with on more than one occasion. She remembered him saying how thrilled he was the last time the husband had gone to jail, and then how disgusted he was when he learned how quickly he had been released. He was already running Code 3 when she got the call from him saying he would be late. He said he loved her three times. It made her uneasy from the second she hung up the phone. They always said it twice, always. Three times could only mean one thing, he knew it could be bad.

She knew she wasn't alone. The others must have thought about it, maybe they would never admit it, but they thought about it. She always assumed the doorbell would ring, that's how she envisioned it, but it was the phone first, and the words she was about to hear, would change her life forever.

They say the initial moments are compared to a tornado in slow motion. She never understood that, even still the words made no sense but she now agreed it was the perfect description. As the reality of what has happened collides with what must be dealt with, coupled with the thoughts of your entire lives swirling in front of your eyes, she felt a mad rush of panic entwined with reflection all at once. A tornado in slow motion. Her mother now on her way to take care of the children and two officers which now stood in her living room eliminated all hope of her denying the truth. Her urge to bolt out the back door and get to the hospital on her own was overwhelming. If there was ever a time she begged her mother to drive like a maniac, it was now. She gently sat on the edge of her son's bed, placed his favorite deputy bear back into his arms and wondered if the next time she saw him she would have to break his heart.

The ride to the hospital was silent, she wanted to ask them but she didn't want to put them in a position to be responsible for telling her, or feel bad for not telling her, so she rode in outward silence while screaming in her own head. She had heard it was bad, there were words spoken that she never wanted to hear. She heard "grave" and "extremely critical" over the radio before she left the house. She knew they knew yet she remained silent for everyone's sake.

She sat in the corridor waiting, one eye on the double doors leading down the hall where they were, one eye on the double doors of the elevator. She had never felt so lost or conflicted. She just kept begging to wake up, "Please dear God, let this be a dream." Just then the double doors opened again, this time it was the elevator. She somehow knew she would be the one to have to break the news.

Why do bad things happen to good people? We've all heard the phrase. But how can horrific, senseless, unimaginable things happen to good people? And how can it possibly happen twice in the same day? She looked into the eyes of his devastated parents and once again begged God to allow her a way out, a way to wake up from this nightmare. Regardless of the outcome, their lives would never be the same.

From the open double doors two doctors emerged, one for each of them. They sat down and closed the door to the little room, looked into her eyes and told her he was fine. He had been shot twice; once in the vest, once in his shoulder. The second doctor explained that more damage was done when his head struck the pavement. He had a bad concussion but would likely be released in a day or so. She began to weep, she buried her head in her lap and wept for the pain she knew was yet to come. She could no longer bear to look at his parents, she had no idea how they could possibly move on from here.

They held hands as they heard the news. "From what the officers explained to us, when your youngest son was shot, he fell to the pavement. He was temporarily unconscious and still in the line of fire. Your oldest son was trying to provide cover for his brother when he was shot. He was shot three times and managed to return fire and kill the suspect before he collapsed. He was literally shooting at the suspect while lying over his brother. Unfortunately he was shot in an artery and lost a tremendous amount of blood. We did all we could, but he did not survive the surgery and we are so sorry for your loss."

How do you have gratitude for what you were spared when those closest to you will suffer eternally? How can you take joy in hearing the words, "Your husband will be fine", when in the same breath you hear his brother died trying to save him? How can you forever be, "The brother that lived?" She sat in the chapel of the hospital completely baffled. She could make no sense of it, and she was angry. She was angry at God for not allowing her to wake up. She had begged Him. She had told Him, "This is too much to bear. How can we ever move on from this?" A touch to her shoulder startled her.

"I'm sorry the doctor's had to tell you, I just wasn't ready to leave him yet. I needed more time to say goodbye." She sat with her sister-in-law in the chapel, they held each other and wept and prayed and wept some more. "I'm so sorry, I can't understand, I don't want to understand, this is all too much."

Her sister-in-law took her hands and said, "We are officer wives and we have children and we are strong, but right now, I am weak. I lost the love of my life here tonight and I have to go home and tell my babies their Daddy is never coming home. And I want to blame God, I want to hate Him for this but right now I have to thank Him. I have to thank Him for sparing Danny. I have to know that it was David's time to go home and it is now Danny's time to protect us. God spared Danny so we could all survive this. I have to believe God knew we needed Danny or this would all be too much to bear. No matter what, we cannot hate God for this and I promise you, I will never hate Danny or you because he lived, or because you have your family. We are forever sisters, but my heart is broken and I need you and Danny to carry me through this. So you see, God is good. God is so very Good. Now...let's go see your husband."

Life without a Safety

In honor of Oklahoma City Police Officer, Chad Peery and Family

It's something we try not to think about, something that is always there, yet rarely spoken out loud. The white elephant in the room, the unspoken thought that screams inside us. Police wives are trained for it, we are molded through experiences to learn to accept it yet not dwell on it. It lurks within all of us, creeps around our forethoughts forming visions in our minds.

As quickly as we realize we are thinking it, seeing it, allowing ourselves to feel it, we dismiss it, bury it, usher it out as quickly as it came. It, is fear.

There's a somewhat ominous feel in the air, more so than usual. Maybe it started a while back in a Lakewood coffee shop, maybe it started before then, but Lakewood was such a shock, such a senseless, murderous rampage of crazed hatred inflicted upon The Lakewood Four. They have a title. Four amazing men and women, with families and lives and hopes and dreams, now summed up in a title reminding us more of the way they were taken from us. A tragedy within a title, yet a reality nonetheless. 2010 proved to be a sad sequel of sorts. We all saw the numbers growing, and growing quickly. We all waited for a lull in the news. It never came.

By December 31st, 2010, we had lost 161. One hundred sixty one officers down. 161 families broken, over 340 children faced with the news Mommy or Daddy was never coming home. Departments across the country buried their brothers and sisters in blue. Wives sat holding their babies trying to grasp their new reality. Parents were left wondering why they had to bury their children. Children were expected to understand what never and forever meant, while accepting that kissing a picture frame at night was the best it would ever be again. And for those of us who were not directly affected by the number 161, we found ourselves doing what we are trained not to do. Worry. Wonder. Wait. LEO wives are trained to be strong, to minimize our fears, to be the backbone of the relationship. We are supposed to be the constant, the present. We are known as the understanding, the accepting, the forgiving, the independent....we are told we are the glue, the voice of reason who can simply say, "I love you, see you later", and train ourselves to believe it will always be true.

We are also human. We are wives, we are mothers, and we are not always strong or fearless of our own voice of reason. In fact, sometimes, we allow ourselves a moment to wish for the option of weakness, or selfishness, or dependency. When trying to wrap our minds around the number 161, I think many of us wished for more than just a moment of weakness. Truth be told, I think many of us wished for the LEO's we love to be our heroes first, and not everyone else's.

A moment. Because in reality, that is all we can afford to take. We all know selfish is not an option, we all know it is life without a safety, we all know; this is it.

We also know, allowing that one moment invites so many emotions we really cannot afford to creep into our minds. So many LEO wives across the country watched the news the day the Lakewood Four fell, and again through 2010 as the number crept to 161, and again when Deputy Sheriff Suzanne Hopper was gunned down in a small German Township on January 1st, 2011. We all hoped 2011 would be different, yet within the first twenty-four days of the new year, fourteen officers and a K-9 were dead. Thirteen officers shot in a mere twenty-four hours. Three officers from St. Petersburg, FL dead within a month.

It's hard to fathom thirty-one officers dying before the end of the first eight weeks of a new year, but that is the reality for 2011. The US is averaging one officer down every two days. More alarming than that statistic, is that of those who survived. Over 60,000 officers were assaulted while on duty in 2010, over 14,000 suffered severe injuries. 2011 has proved no better.

In the first sixty days of 2011, over 12,500 officers have been assaulted and thirty-one have died in the line of duty. One injury that hits particularly close to home is Officer Chad Peery.

On February 15, 2011 at about 10:15pm, off-duty Oklahoma City police officer Chad Peery was watching an OKC Thunder basketball game with family at a local restaurant. He was asked by the staff, who knew he was a police officer, to help escort several belligerent men outside. In the process of doing so, he was brutally attacked and beaten unconscious by the men, who then fled the scene. He was taken to the hospital where it was discovered he had a broken neck and is paralyzed.

Officer Peery is the father of four children. He and his entire family are facing a long-term, possibly lifelong struggle, both emotionally and financially. Chad's life changed forever in a split second. His decision to help, even off duty, was surprising to none. It proved once again, nothing is routine but some things are constant, like the impeccable character of a good officer.

Officers are faced with constant scrutiny from the public. The fact remains, crimes committed by corrupt officers, including deaths, assaults, sexual assaults and other acts, albeit disturbing, make up less than two percent of all officers in this country. It is no coincidence that the majority of those who voice their hatred for the police are those who are involved in illegal activity, have an establish criminal record or are living a life which is not conducive to a life abiding by those laws which our law enforcement officers try to maintain and uphold. Approximately 63,000 police officers were assaulted in 2010. Yet, there were less than 6,700 reports of police misconduct in the United States last year, over 60% of which were attributed to unsubstantiated excessive force or sexual misconduct complaints.

As any officer, or any person who watches one episode of COPS can attest, almost every arrest made involves a suspect making some form of accusation that the officers used excessive force and there's not an officer out there who doesn't have a "drunk Sally" story of the regular DUI stop which involves the drunk female throwing out threats and complaints of being sexually assaulted or beaten by an officer. For those with legitimate complaints, they deserve justice. For those officers who abuse their power, there is no excuse. They deserve no better than the criminals of a similar nature.

But for the overwhelming amount that are good cops, those who honor the badge and uphold their duty as officers with integrity, they are our heroes.

71

Just as our troops protect us abroad, protecting our freedom from distant borders, there is the tragic, occasional incident of friendly fire, the death of civilians and even the corrupt soldiers, although few and far between, but there, inflicting injustice on innocent residents of towns with no powers against them. Still, we honor our troops. We fly our flags for them, we offer our unconditional support for them, we parade them upon their return to our soil, we line our airports with love and salutes and honor for them. For those soldiers injured we go above an beyond to offer our support and show our appreciation for their duty, sacrifices and dedication to protecting our freedom, as we should.

Our police officers deserve the same. They are our protectors, the peace keepers of our borders and streets. There is no one else to do their job, no one else who will do their job. You can have a criminal record a mile long, they can know you by name, by gang affiliation, by reputation, or lack thereof. You can yell at them, spit at them, threaten them and call them worthless PIGS one day, but dial 911 the next and they will still come. They begin each shift knowing that same cop hater they are rushing to help could try and make today a day another cop dies. They know every day could be their last. They know what 161 in 2010 means, but it will not define them, or deter them, or shake them. They know nothing is routine. They think twice before entering a coffee shop now, although more so for the safety of the patrons and employees. They are more alert inside their own substations, as even they are still wrapping their heads around Detroit.

Those lucky enough to work in low crime areas who used to wonder about the excitement and dangers known to officers in the big cities think about Chad Peery, enjoying a basketball game at a local restaurant in the good part of town. They understand the increase, they feel it, but just like Chad Peery, that knowledge will never stop them from their call of duty, whether they are on the clock or not, for they are called to protect and serve, it is who they are, it is never just a job to them. Our police officers begin every shift ready and willing to lay down their life for any given stranger at any given moment. They are dedicated to protecting and serving their communities, regardless of the lack of support received from those they protect. Our officers deserve our respect and support.

I have said it before, there must be an awakening in America. Our officers are losing their lives to repeat, violent offenders who have been released back onto our streets time and time again. Our laws are failing our officers. Overcrowding and budget cuts are emptying our prisons and filling our communities with felons while police jobs are being cut across the country. We have less officers, more criminals and a negative perception of law enforcement which fuels the violent tendencies of those with nothing to lose. When you can assault a police officer and be released early, what is the deterrent from doing it again? When you hate the police anyway, why not aim to get the job done the next time?

Our officers need our support. American's need to be aware of the true statistics of good versus evil in law enforcement. There were over 630,000 fully commissioned law enforcement officers in the Unites States in 2010 and less than 10,000 reports of cases involving police corruption and crime. Over half a million officers, less than 10,000 complaints. Until we begin to treat our officers as the heroes they truly are and until our laws mandate they receive the respect they deserve by imposing harsh sentences with no parole or early release options for those who assault our officers, and life sentences for those who kill our officers, the violence upon our officers will continue.

The three individuals who assaulted Chad Peery knew he was a police officer. That's all it took. One held him, one beat him and one worked to keep patrons from coming to his aid. They are a prime example of those members of society who not only have no respect for others, but possess a blatant disregard for human life and an open hatred for our officers. It is men such as these who are hunting and assassinating our officers.

Chad Peery is a hero, he is what being a police officer is all about. He is a testament that officers live their lives on duty, there is never a time they are not compelled to protect and serve. I hope the Oklahoma justice system holds the individuals accountable and uses this senseless tragedy to at least make it clear that in Oklahoma, when you bring down an officer, you will never taste freedom again. How absolutely sickening that this is the circumstance in which we have to have that hope. Chad and his family deserve so much more than that.

And so we begin another day, and the LEO wives strive on. We will not allow the numbers to shake our faith, we will take a deep breath when we see the news, we will say another prayer when they walk out the door and we will thank God every time they walk back in. We will remind ourselves a little more often why we live the way we do, so our LEO's can head off into the night with focus and determination to make it back home. We will rededicate ourselves daily to focus on the good our husbands do while they are out protecting others, we will push aside any selfish tendencies and recommit ourselves to being the wives our LEO's need. Before we entertain that next moment of selfishness or weakness or we allow that fear to creep into our thoughts, we will remind ourselves that each day is a blessing, and any moment could be a turning point.

Be grateful for our officers.

What Might Have Been

"This was a huge mistake," she said to herself. She sat, silently, the occasional nod of acknowledgment, the quick smile, the gesture of agreement, all the while she was soaking in the moment like a sponge, absorbing every last drop of shallowness as if to be a reminder when she starting having pangs of the other side's view of "normalcy."

Ten years prior as she walked the path between the dorms and Central Hall she noticed him, noticing her. His eyes clearly locked as he pretended to study a text book. "Why are you looking at him?" "He's looking at me, I'm not looking at him," she quickly replied to her best friend, although she knew she was not fooling anyone. "Good, because there's no point in looking at a pretty package that can't afford to be wrapped, if you know what I mean. He's studying Criminal Justice, my brother knows him. And not for something cool like the FBI or something, he wants to be a cop." She didn't even bother speaking up about what a shallow statement that was, after all, it would never matter anyway, she was headed to law school in three years, she heard he was a senior.

"Why can't I ever get anywhere on time?" Frustrated at the clock once again she vented out loud. "For someone who plans on getting to court on time every day, you better figure it out Missy." As usual, her bestie had a way of kicking her self-esteem that last little way into the gutter. "I'll make it to court on time when I'm a lawyer, you can't compare a party to my future life in litigation." "Whatever, Legal Eagle, get your shoes on for God's sake, we're totally missing the first band."

This was not her scene. She never knew why she let herself be talked into these things. She really hated crowds, the music was always too loud, there was always a crowd of drunks acting like idiots. Once again she found herself wishing she would have just stayed at home to study. She had to get away from the stench of cigarette smoke and sweat. She knew she wouldn't be missed either.

"This is a good way to get yourself killed, you know." She jumped at least two feet straight up and off the park bench she had planted herself on outside the club. "Oh my God, are you &%#^% crazy? You scared me to death!" Realizing she had just cussed out a police officer didn't even worry her at that point.

"Sorry, I didn't mean to scare you to death, I was just trying to point out there are better options if you would like to stay alive." He said it so matter of fact like. "How are you going to sneak up on someone like that without scaring them to death, really?!" she replied. "Actually, I'm pretty much trained to sneak up on people, it's not a personal thing against you, just to be clear." His response came with more than a tad bit of sarcasm.

She had moved down the sidewalk now, closer to the entrance of the little dive that was known as the campus hot spot on the weekends. The light from the street lamp revealed his face to her and she knew she had seen him before. "Do I know you?" She asked as she wracked her memory. "We went to school together. You used to have a crush on me, you were just younger and forgot about it." He said it with complete cattiness she found rather intriguing. "Excuse me, but I don't recall going to school with you and I certainly would not forget if I were attracted to you and believe me, I have no recollection of either whatsoever," she responded with her intellectually superior law student voice. "So, I just look familiar for no apparent reason, is that what you're telling me?"

He loved getting a little dig in already, he could tell her personality was one who loved to hate it. "Well, I see you're fitting of that uniform, already interrogating me for asking a simple question, I see how it is." "I wouldn't have to interrogate you at all if you would just admit to what we both already know. We went to school together, you had a crush on me, your friends thought I was a loser and you never gave me a second thought."

She looked at him for a moment, studied him. He looked so handsome in that uniform, although, being the perfectionist she posed to be, she already noticed his shirt was worn from the leather of his gun belt, she noticed what appeared to be yesterday's five o'clock shadow masking his very pretty jawline. Actually, he looked very tired to her if the truth be known. Something about him softened her. "Well actually, if you must know, I did give you a second thought. I just didn't listen very well back then."

"Do you think we'll ever get to sleep in, together?" She lay on his chest, whispering in his ear as if trying to make a place for two in a bed filled with four. "You have Cheerios in your hair" he said as he flicked a piece of cereal off of her hair onto the floor. She held on just a minute longer, ignoring the toddlers who loved to turn their king sized bed into a bouncy house on Saturday mornings. She ignored it because she had learned to cherish it. Regardless of the chaos amongst her, she clung to each memory made which included him.

"Daddy, do you have to go get the bad guys again?" The words she wished were not spoken were spoken for her out of the mouth of innocence. "Yes, baby, Daddy has to go to work." "So, that phone call the other day, what are you planning to do about it?" he asked. She really didn't know what she would do about it. She really had no idea why, after 10 years, her old best friend from college would have called her to begin with. After all, she left the sorority, never finished law school. She didn't exactly follow in her friends' footsteps. So why she would be asked to be on the reunion committee was frankly, beyond her. "I really don't know. I just don't see the point. It's not like I could plan to do anything like that with your schedule anyway." That was an easy excuse and a certain way not to face her past. "I think you should do it. My mom can help. You need to do something for yourself, this is a great reason. You can catch up with all your "BFF's" right, get all dolled up, go show them all how good you turned out." She silently cringed at the thought of justifying her life to the superficial past she used to proudly call her own. "We'll see. You better get up. You're going to be late."

"Have I not left my house in the last decade? Where are all my good clothes? This is crazy, I couldn't go to a funeral if I wanted to, much less a brunch." She started running over a million excuses to get out of the luncheon: kids are sick, husband got called out, you name it, she could make it happen. But there was something calling her there. Perhaps it was curiosity, wondering who gained weight, who married whom, who had children, who had managed to pay off their student loans, but in all honesty she knew what was calling her there. She wanted to know. She desired to know, just for her own sake, what it could have been like. Had she finished law school, had she followed the path of her college friends, had she made her parents proud by carrying on the family tradition of law. She never did understand why marrying an officer didn't get her credit for that in a way. No one understood really, and she understood that clearly.

She grabbed her keys and her emergency cash and headed for the local discount store. She had exactly two hours before preschool was over and she was going to find something to wear to make her fit in.

"Why am I feeling like a garbage man in this minivan?" She pulled up to the Valet hoping to God no one was watching. As she looked around a parking lot filled with Range Rover's, BMW's, Benz' and Bentley's she realized she was out of her league. She felt the need to ditch her faux Coach bag and hide her Ford key fob. As she approached the hostess she heard shrills coming from the side room of the restaurant. "Oh my Gawd, look at you, you look amazing, come see everyone!" She was already looking forward to the end of this luncheon.

A full hour into conversations concerning horrible mothers at private school, you know who, sleeping with you know who, where to get the best Botox, which trial lawyers have which judges in their pockets and which couples therapist is the best to see after your pet therapist. She felt her sense of insecurity fading quickly. She felt a sense of anger coming over her. She felt a sense of sorrow that some of the most educated people truly had no regard for what mattered most. She felt a sense of defeat while strangely coupled with a sense of pride and defensiveness for her husband and her life, and its simplicity and it's worth.

"So, Ally, you've been very quiet over there, tell us what you've been up to," her former "bestie" asked of her. It became very clear in that tone, in that manner, after all the stature which predicated her request, she understood she was there as a mockery. She was very familiar with her family being a mockery. Today, she would not be a mockery any longer.

"What have I been up to? Well, you all know what I have been up to. I married the love of my life eight years ago. We have twin boys. My husband is a police officer. I never finished law school. Our life was so grueling, I chose to stay home and spend as much time with my husband as I could, because I feared everyday might be my last with him. I had children knowing I might raise them alone. I spend almost every night alone. I rarely see my husband on my birthday. We celebrate Christmas on the 27th, we celebrate Father's Day on Tuesday and Mother's Day on Wednesday. I sleep with my cell phone on my pillow and pray it never rings. I can drink a bottle of wine and take a sleeping pill and still hear the garage door as soon as it begins to open."

"I raise my children alone while explaining to them the parent who is mostly invisible is a bigger hero than I could ever be. I cook dinner at 3:00am and lunch at 5:00pm and it still sits uneaten most of the time. I worry each time I hear a siren or a breaking news alert that my husband is dead. I watch a brute of a man with a heart of an angel come into my home unable to speak of the horrors he has seen and smelled and remembers no matter how much he tries to drink or sleep or shower the memories away.

I look at people who live a life of luxury and complain of such things as a bad apple-tini or a piss poor room at the Palms in Vegas or the fact that their maid didn't dust the baseboards and I cringe. I listen to stories of marriages in demise over other women and men because of selfish greed and want and excess and I want to shake you all. What have I been up to? I have been up to it all."

"I have been up to it and faced it and dealt with it and overcome it and persevered through it and striven past it and continue to live with it and more than anything I rejoice in it. And do you know why? Because I know what matters in life, that's why. I know what love is really all about and I know what cherishing life is about and I know what it is to live in fear that each day you wake up might be the last day of happiness as you know it. And none of that costs a dime or requires a degree or a perfect credit score. What have I been up to? I, have been living the good life."

She picked up her faux Coach purse and the parking ticket to claim her minivan and she walked out.

"How did your lunch thing go?" he asked while she listened over the squawk of the radio in the background.

"It was fine, I think they can handle everything without me. I didn't eat there, though. Do you want to meet at our usual place?"

"You know, that's a good way to get yourself killed," he said with a smirk in his voice. "It's not exactly a good part of town for a cute girl like you to be hanging out in a parking lot."

"It's okay," she said, "I know people who can keep me alive."

"So, I keep you alive, huh?"

"More than you could ever know," she said. "You want fries or onion rings?"

"Surprise me, baby."

Life is good.

And Life Goes On

Perhaps it was exhaustion, she couldn't remember when she last slept. Perhaps it was just being at her own limits, pushed well beyond what anyone should have to cope with. Whatever it was, she found herself there, not being able to shake the image of Sally Fields in Steel Magnolias holding Julia Roberts hand at her bedside. "Open your eyes Shelby, open your eyes!" Was it wrong to laugh on the inside at a time like this? After all the crying she had done over the past week, she felt Dr. Phil and Oprah and at least three out of four therapists would agree she needed to laugh again.

She did what she had done for the past six days, sat at his side, held his hand, talked to him about how their son's soccer game went, how their oldest daughter won second place in the science fair, thanks to him and his ability to create a contained explosive device inside a Tupperware container; bomb squad did have its perks after all. Oh, and about Buddy, who dug his way into the neighbor's yard and terrorized their basset hound again. Not that he heard a word of what she was saying, but that's what you're supposed to do, right? Talk to them like everything is going to be fine. It was not fine, and on the inside she was not fine. On the inside, she was dying.

Six times a day. That's how many times the specialist team would come in to see him. Six times a day she held her breath. Six times a day she wondered if the tests would tell a change in the tide. She had been trained to expect the worst and hope for the best. She had become accustomed to the unknown. She certainly was no stranger to fear or anxiety or stress or maintaining independently. So why…why did she feel so ill prepared for this? She knew the answer. As she looked at her husband, laying there lifeless yet alive, clinging to this world by machines and tubes and drains and monitors and air that was not his own and a heart that no longer beat by itself, she knew why she was so ill prepared for this. She realized at that moment for the past fourteen years she had trained herself for the knock at the door, but she had been prepared for him to die, not for him to live.

She felt like a horrible person. So many people, total strangers, sending cards and flowers and donations, news crews at the hospital day in, day out. Facebook and Twitter pages set up by people she had never met, all in support of her and her husband and their family. She just wanted it all to go away. It was too much and she had never asked for this. All she did was answer the phone. This wasn't supposed to be her. This was never supposed to happen to her family.

Everything was finally good. They had made it past the night shift, they made it past the kids being babies, they had made it past the years of crazy schedule changes and department politics and they had paid their dues. Doesn't that count for anything? Doesn't that entitle me, she asked herself? She didn't know why she tortured herself with what ifs…after all, what ifs would be around for the rest of her life now. She shook herself back to the reality of the moment. Specialist visit number three for the day. Maybe they would tell her how to raise three kids and an unruly dog from a hospital room. That, she thought, would make them specialists.

"You need to eat something, you're wasting away in here." Her mother-in-law always did have a way with words. She felt that horrible person syndrome creeping back to the surface. She had a routine. Once she arrived at the hospital after taking the kids to school, she didn't leave his side until she went to pick them up from school and bring them to the hospital. It was bad enough that his parents were essentially raising her children now, truth be told, she would never have chosen her mother-in-law for any child raising duties under normal circumstances. The thought of taking the most simple of suggestions about eating from her mother-in-law frankly almost made laser beams shoot from her own eyes. Of course, if it would save having to hear her trying to convince her to eat a panini for another hour, it was probably easier to just go get a sandwich.

Looking at the time, she realized it was actually good timing. If she left now, she would miss specialist visit number four completely.

The execs at this restaurant are geniuses, she thought as she stood in line. She had never noticed that this chain was across the street from every single hospital until she found herself living at one. She found herself feeling awkwardly out of place in a sea of scrubs and white coats. There was that sarcasm again. No better time to choke on a sandwich than now, she thought. She made her way to the farthest corner by the bathrooms and sat. She sat, alone.

She had no more than taken the first bite of her sandwich as she noticed a mother and a clearly sick little girl rushing toward the bathroom. Trying not to stare as they hurried by, the little girl rushed inside yelling, "I can do it myself!" Issues, she thought, as the bathroom door slammed followed by the sound of vomiting and water splashing coming from behind the closed door. No longer able to ignore the un-ignorable, she looked up at the young mother, standing against the bathroom door, her forehead resting on the doorframe, her hand pressed against the door. Oh my God, she looks like hell, she thought to herself, perhaps realizing her expression spoke what her mind was thinking just as the young mother's eyes caught hers. "She has cancer. I'm sorry if that ruined your appetite, you just never know about the nausea." "Oh, it's fine, I have three kids, I know all about vomit." Well...that didn't come out right. They both laughed just for a second, slightly awkward, but a clearly understood moment between mothers. "Are you alright honey?" "I'm FINE, leave me alone!" came from behind the bathroom door.

"Wow, that must be really rough, I'm really sorry." Was that compassion she just heard coming from her own mouth? "It's alright, we've been dealing with this for six years, she's normally very sweet, she just really wanted to eat here and you never know when the nausea will come back. It hits her at the wrong times, always, and besides, we've been through way worse than vomit. I'm sorry, you are clearly trying to eat here and I'm monopolizing your lunch hour, I'm sure. We'll be out of here in just a minute." The mother pressed her ear up to the bathroom door again. "Are you almost done in there?"

"You are fine, seriously, I'm not on my lunch hour anyway, I'm just...here." She noticed the mother's wedding set, it was very nice. At least she has help, she thought to herself. The little girl emerged from

93

the bathroom, her hot pink bandana tied around her bald head, the back clearly soaked with sweat. Her cheeks were red and swollen. As she looked closer she noticed needle marks and scars and medical tape all over her. She realized she was staring. "I hope you feel better real soon." That's all I can come up with? she thought to herself.

She watched as they left and saw them grab hands as they walked to their car. She felt a sense of lacking creep up into her throat. Tears began to flow as she thought about her children and what they were feeling and thinking. She started to acknowledge for the first time what she was thinking and feeling . She was mad. She was angry at her husband for getting shot in the head. She hated to admit it to herself, but it was true. She knew she had to get a hold of herself for her own sake, and her children. She threw her panini in the trash and headed to her car.

She didn't really know why she pushed the elevator button to the second floor. She was never really a praying kind of person. She believed in God, but praying...actually praying, really? She had never felt compelled before now. As she entered the hospital chapel she saw the same mother kneeling, weeping. "I'm sorry, I'm not stalking you, I swear. I just..."

The mother interrupted her mid-sentence, saying, "Do you want to pray with me?" She was completely caught off guard. She didn't even pray, and now this mother from the restaurant with a kid who had cancer was here in the chapel and was asking if she wanted to pray? Who does this? For whatever reason, she felt like now, right now, she does this. Every emotion from the past week washed over her. All the emotions of terror and fear and confusion and denial and pain and yes, anger, lots and lots of anger washed over her right at that very minute. By God if there was a God, yes. Yes, she wanted to pray and she wanted to pray with this total stranger she had never met before they had just shared vomit and a panini and for whatever reason they now shared this chapel so yes, she wanted to pray, now.

"Yes." She cried as the woman took her hands in her own. "Who are you praying for?"

She could barely speak, because speaking meant saying it, and saying it meant acknowledging it. "My husband, he's a police officer...and last Thursday they shot him in the head... these thugs, they just... I

95

have three kids and he's hanging on but no one will tell me if he'll live and I'm just so scared."

The woman looked into her eyes with purpose and squeezed her hands and said, "You can do this, I promise, you can do this." And she began to pray. "Dear Heavenly Father, I ask that you be with my sister, I ask that you give her strength to get through this time. I ask that you give her faith in you Lord, I ask that you protect her children and give them peace at this time, I ask that you give them the understanding and patience and guidance and ability to give this to you Lord, to let your will be done. And I ask for a miracle God. I ask you to bring total healing to her husband and bring him through this injury completely. Give him the strength to recover and the strength to dedicate himself to the recovery process."

She paused, took a deep breath, squeezed her hands tighter and continued, "And Lord, should it be your will that he not survive, I ask that you make his transition to Heaven peaceful. And Lord I ask should this brother be brought home early to you, that you have my husband there to meet him and guide him and help him through the gates, in your name I pray, Amen."

She looked into the eyes of the woman and realized what God had done that day. They both realized it. She didn't know what to say. "I lost my Officer two years ago," the young mother said. "What are the chances this would happen like this?"

The young mother looked at her and said, "Unfortunately, lately the chances are a lot more likely than they used to be."

Five years later as they sat on the beach they both looked up at the same time as a screaming little boy went running down the beach, his mother chasing behind him as well as she could keep up. The boy stopped dead in his tracks and emptied his stomach of what was clearly an entire day's worth of hot dogs, ice cream, salt water and too much sun.

They both looked at each other and laughed hysterically, at the same time announcing their sister motto: "BEEN THERE, DONE THAT!!"

And life goes on.

An Officer's POV

I am a Police Officer

I am a police officer.

I have sworn to protect life and property, deter crime and serve my community.

I have answered a calling that few can answer. I do a job that few can do and fewer understand.

I stand upon a line drawn in the darkness that separates good and evil.

I live my life to a higher degree of moral and ethical standards, not because I have to but because I choose too.

I sacrifice time with my family and friends for complete strangers.

I wear Kevlar and feel naked without it.

I gaze upon my town through the windshield of my car, not looking at the good in it, but looking for the bad in it.

I look out for you and protect you and you do not realize what that means.

I am ridiculed, second guessed and made fun of by young and old alike, knowing that those same people will call for me when they need help.

I am spit upon, assaulted and killed while serving others. Yet I continue to serve you.

I am witness to the most evil acts a person can do to another yet am expected to perform my duties flawlessly.

If a business is robbed, it is my fault for not doing my job.

If you have something stolen from your car, it's my fault, I should have been on your street. I don't care if you blame me, I have broad shoulders and will gently point out to you that you should not leave valuables in your car at night.

I will come to your house day after day and referee your domestic and when I take your partner away to jail, I will watch as you post their bail and take them home again.

I will investigate your crash and gather up your belongings and make sure they get to the hospital with you and listen to you complain the next day that something is missing.

I will listen as you tell me you pay my salary and you will have my badge while I silently wish I could tell you I need a raise and that you are not man/woman enough to take my badge.

I will come to your house because you can't control your eight year old child and talk to them for you because you do not know how.

I want to get business cards that say discipline is not abuse, try it. And I want to hand them out to people, but I cannot do that.

I laugh at you when you try and sneak your seatbelt on while you drive in front of me.

When I get back in my car from talking to people I shake my head in disbelief at what they tell me.

I do not enjoy blocking the road and standing in the hot sun or freezing cold or pouring rain directing traffic. I do not do it just to piss you off, there is a reason for it. Deal with it.

I have feelings. I have good days and bad days, I work when I am sick so I don't short my shift.

I would not trade my job for any other in the world. I am a police officer and I love it.

His Name is Leo

She was nineteen years old. The world was hers. She had waited for three years. She remembered high school like it was yesterday. She remembered seeing him, all six feet, two inches of his gorgeous frame walking down the hall, straight towards her locker, making a beeline to her, making his intentions crystal clear. She had known him since kindergarten, she had make believe plans for their future for years. The future was now. They had been together since the eighth grade, she was protective from the start.

She always felt this sense, that everyone wanted a piece of him. She couldn't put her finger on it, but she had always felt he belonged to someone else, or maybe she just never felt he belonged just to her. For whatever reason, she stood by him, she fought to belong to him. She had no idea at the time the gravity of what was to come, but as she would look back years later, she would come to realize....she was never first in line. Something greater would always have a hold on him.

She was twenty two. She was adjusted. They had made it through academy and the adjustments of the first few years of life in law enforcement. She had it down to a science now. She knew when a call didn't come it would be at least two hours. She knew not to keep dinner on the stove. She knew, even as small as he was, to prepare their son that Daddy would be home later and would come and see him when he could. She got it. She was used to it. And she could tell the difference between a normal shift and a bad shift. She knew what it was all about.

As she took a washcloth to the cold water she thought to herself, "I'm going to end up doing this alone, I just know it." She was near her breaking point with the pain, and the nausea was almost too much to bear. She fumbled about the kitchen, her little boy under her feet. "I need more juice, Mommy." "I know, Son, I know." Her contractions getting stronger, she continued to breathe through the pain. She gave her son his sippy cup. "Nappy time." "I don't want to take a nap." She knew it wasn't even time for his nap, but it was the only way. Amazingly enough, it was as if he knew; Mommy could take no more. She then focused her attention on her contractions and the phone calls which had to be made.

Her thoughts kept taking her back to the football field, those days where he was always there. The simple days where love was love and nothing in this world could ever come between them; even then, she had a feeling, call it a premonition, call it intuition, nonetheless, she knew somehow, for some reason, her life would be different.

He never answered. He never did. Today should not surprise her. He barely made it to the birth of their first child, why would she expect anything different this time. She called her mother. Panicked over her travel arrangements, as it was a full three weeks early, she now questioned her own sanity in calling her mother. She tried texting him, calling him -

nothing. Seven minutes apart. Seven minutes. Seven minutes. She sat on the side of the bed, rocking herself through the pain. "What am I going to do…oh God, why…what am I going to do." She found herself as she always did - alone. In love, in a supportive marriage, a wife with a loving husband who was just as excited about this child as she was, and yet, she was alone. She was almost always alone. It was the life. It was just a part of her reality. And here she was, for the second time, believing, somehow, someway, he would get her message, he would break free from whatever call had his attention, he would get there. Somehow he would get there, and they would have that makeshift moment they had learned to call, "family time."

Tears rolled down her face as she began to push. No one would say it. No one wanted her to know it. She knew. She felt him leave her. She knew if he were with her, he would be there. Regardless of the duty, the call, the circumstance, she knew. If she needed him, really needed him, the way only he knew and understood she needed him. If he were here, he would be there for her.

She knew he was gone as she gave up the fight to hold on to him. She knew if their child began to come into this world without him, it was because he was already on the other side, a guardian watching over them. No one would tell her. No one had to. As a room filled with anguish fought to bring her support, she held back her sorrow for the sake of her own mother, her father, her son, her beloved's parents. She did what she was trained to do. She was the wife of an officer. She was strong. She was brave. She put others before herself. She allowed them to live for just a few hours longer without facing the truth she had felt for hours before.

As they laid her newborn son on her chest, the room erupted in a mix of anguished joy, she looked into the eyes of his parents, she felt their pain, the loss that had yet to be spoken for her sake. She looked into their eyes as she announced he would be named after his father. A hero, a father, a son, a brother. As they wept she remembered that day, so long ago, the two of them on the bleachers, so in love, so much ahead of them, she remembered that conversation where he said, "I hope we have a whole bunch of kids someday...I don't know why, but I love the name Leo."

Nothing Lasts Forever

It was the closest thing to heaven she could experience. She stood there on the porch, looked out into eternity, inhaled as deeply as she could, taking in the ocean breeze. This was her 'once in a blue moon' and she cherished every second of it. As she gazed out past the sand, off into the sea, she found herself having to push all the normal thoughts away. Even here, even now, as beautiful as it was, as safe as it was, it was still temporary. "Nothing lasts forever," she caught herself whispering.

"I'm going for a quick run," he said as he kissed her on the cheek. She gave him a quick smile and watched him head off down the beach. Still running barefoot, after all these years, she couldn't help but smile as he faded off into the distance. Her eyes wandered back to the porch, taking in the moment.

She had done it for years now, yet it never became old. She loved memorizing and re-memorizing every inch of the little beach house they rented for a week each year. It wasn't luxurious or even fussy, it was just simple perfection. It was a week, a full seven days and six nights of peace each year, away from the chaos of their not so normal life. It was a full week for them to reconnect with each other, but more than anything, what mattered the most to her at least, was a full week of days and nights where she had no concerns for his safety, she slept in his arms, she was awakened by the warmth of the sun and his body next to hers.

All of that, together with the crash of the waves, the smell of sand and sea - it was almost too much for her at times. Just now, she found herself coming back to reality as she heard herself say it again, "Nothing lasts forever." Time for some breakfast, he'll be back soon.

"Do you realize this is the fourteenth summer we've come here?" he said as they lay there, entwined like pretzels, looking past the gauze curtains which ushered in the ocean air. He was holding her, the way he really only did that one week a year, the week he let himself be more human than he could ever allow himself to normally be.

"Do you realize how many times we've made love here?" she said as he kissed her neck while they looked out at the sun coming up over the horizon, lighting up the ocean like a rainbow of color and movement dancing toward the shore. "We should probably get up and do something," she said. "Well, that would be a waste, now wouldn't it?" She remembered why she fell in love with him to begin with; this man…this man who seemed to only exist in bits and pieces and moments here and there during her entire marriage, but who seemed to emerge in magnitude for that one short week every year. In a way, it kept her going. Knowing the love he was capable of, knowing why it seemed to remain suppressed for much of their lives together, but knowing still, it was there.

Given the right circumstance, that man that was capable of giving himself to her, emotionally, physically, without limits, was there.   That moment, the way it happened every year, as he returned from his early morning run on the beach, snuck up behind her and told her to turn off the stove. It was their tradition, just as it was to look out at the ocean as the sun began to rise and play its rays onto the sea, this was them. As much as she loved every moment of this week, this feeling of security and safety she felt with his arms wrapped around her, she said it anyway, "Nothing lasts forever, we should probably get up and make the most of today."

He abruptly got up and headed for the shower. She said nothing. She knew she had done it again. For as much as he tried to give her what she needed, for as much as he tried to let himself be human for that one week, for as much as he tried to forget being a cop, it wasn't enough for her.   She knew it. She realized why he walked away. She lived her life, fifty-one weeks a year, being the wife of an officer. She put on a brave front, she took on the majority of the family responsibilities, she raised their children, she did what every other officer's wives did, she lived life single and supportive, all the while she slowly built up a wall of protection around herself. Over the years as she watched officers die horrible and early deaths she prepared herself for the worst. Each close call her husband had she would push through her own terror and take on the persona of the strong LEO wife. "Nothing lasts forever," she would say, and thank God for yet one more day, all the while expecting fully that tomorrow would never come.

He could feel her distance through her support and it weighed on him. To know the dangers he faced, the unknown he headed out into each shift, the moments over his twenty six years of service where he wasn't sure he would make it until tomorrow...she had lived it all, and it had molded her into who she was today. She loved him. She loved him so much, yet she had convinced herself in order to protect herself that she should be prepared that tomorrow would most likely not come for her. She never wanted to be one of the wives who couldn't handle that knock at the door.

But she knew...she knew it had made her cold, it had made her unfeeling, it had made her the LEO wife who was waiting for her husband to die, and not the LEO wife making the most out of every moment he lived.

"I'm sorry," she said as she wrapped her arms around his waist, the warm water of the shower masking her tears. "I'm sorry too. This is really all my fault. I think I did this to you. I try to show you-"

She interrupted him, "It's not your fault, I did this to myself."

"I've only got two years to retirement, the worst is over. I'm not going anywhere, I've told you for twenty five years." He begged her to hear him.

"You just don't know how much I love you," she said. He held her as she wept in his arms until the water ran cold.

She promised him that day, she promised herself that day that she would live. She would live her life and embrace his. No matter what happened she knew she had to let him go. Let him go while he was still with her. Let him be free from guilt and worry and the pain of feeling he had caused this over the years. She wasn't perfect, she had her moments, but she resigned herself to reality. He may not come home and she could never change that whether she enjoyed her life day to day or not.

One year later.

"I'm going for a quick run, come with me?" She was so taken aback she didn't think she had heard him correctly.

"You want me…to run with you?"

"C'mon, I have something to show you."

"I don't have any running shoes," she said, still completely puzzled.

"I've run on this beach for fifteen years now with no shoes, take a risk, what do you have to lose, right?"

"Alright, you got me there….I guess breakfast can wait."

"We've never eaten breakfast right after I run, anyway, now have we?" She couldn't help but smile at that one.

They headed off down the beach, a path she had never once, in fifteen years traveled with him. His run was his time for himself, she never asked where he ran, or how far, it was just her way of knowing he needed to keep up with his stamina for the next week, when he returned to his reality.

"Close your eyes," he said, as he stopped running and placed his hands over her eyes from behind her.

"What are you doing?" she asked as she put her hands up to his as he held her from behind.

"I have a surprise for you." He let his hands away from her eyes while still holding her hands.

The house was beautiful: quaint, but spectacular, with a deck that wrapped around the entire house. Just steps from the water, private, the houses on either side were an eternity apart. The view was incredible, no sand dunes, no public access, it was a dream come true for a vacation rental.

"What is this? Are you changing our tradition? I love our little beach house, I don't want to change it after all this time. Plus, this must be twice as much to rent for a week in the summer!"

"Shhh," he said, gently putting his finger up to her mouth. He handed her a pretty little satin pouch he had tucked into his waistband.

"What is this?" she asked. She opened the drawstring and a brass key fell out into her hand. Completely puzzled she looked at him in question.

"The house is yours. I've looked at it every single time I ran for the past fifteen years."

"But, what about your job? You have one year left! What about our house? What about...everything? What have you done?"

"It's called early retirement. I figured it's time I do what you've been doing for the past year. It's time to live. And besides, we better make the best of growing old together. You know...nothing lasts forever."

The Answer is Yes

I'm writing this to answer what some have asked me. The answer is yes. I do get overwhelmed, I do get discouraged. I do feel defeated at times. It tears me apart to have us all laughing and enjoying our day with each other, with our families, and within five minutes our world can turn completely upside down.

What other "family" or "community" or "group" or whatever you want to call "us" has to deal with the circumstances we do? How many others send their spouses off, day after day, not knowing if it is the last time you would ever see them alive? Not knowing each time you pick up the phone or hang up the phone if it is a call either beginning the change of your world forever, or ending a world you have always known?

What others think of death in the back of their minds each time they hear a siren, each time they get an unexplained chill, each time there's a second, a twinge of something, something you can't even put your finger on, but something that makes you grab your phone instantly and begs for there to be an answer?

What others have no one else to understand this life other than us who live it? Everyone has someone to turn to? Everyone has family who understands, best friends who will always lend an ear, people close to them they can always turn to for support? No? What others have to turn to a community of those whom they have never met to find some source of comfort in times of anguish because for some reason the death we experience is considered a part of a job description? Who else has to defend and explain and justify why death within their world is devastating and real and not ordinary? Who else has to beg for a simple understanding that their pain is real, that their spouses are human, that being ambushed and executed and point blank murdered is not a standard risk of the job? Who else would ever have to defend that?

Who else lives life being hated for trying to protect those who hate them? Who else is hated and dismissed and shrugged off and discounted for being married to someone who lives life trying to protect others? Who else endures the daily struggles of raising our children alone, being lonely, having plans upset, having holidays with no time for celebration?

Who else is consistently questioned about our poor choice of mate should we ever complain about the life we have chosen....after all, we signed up for this, and it's all just a part of the job.

The answer is yes. Yes I cry, yes I am sad, yes I want to give up, yes I say "F you" to them under my breath. Yes I get tired of being positive. Yes, I get sick of being supportive. Yes, I resent those that hate him having more of him than I ever will. Yes, I hate it all at certain times. Yes, I just want to take him and run with him and my children and never look back at this life which keeps him dangling on a thread being held by a God who seems to allow the thread to continually slip out of his hands. Yes, I get angry and want to say, no more.

No...I will not give in to those emotions. No, I will not allow my perfectly normal human nature to ever be stronger then the LEO wife I vowed to be, as the LEO wife in me requires me to be stronger than just human nature. No, I will never let them win. No, I will not give up, I will not stop believing in change. No, I will not allow myself to become resentful and petty and selfish and self-serving at the expense of my husband's happiness. No, I will not allow myself to lose sight of the actual source of all of my negative emotions: evil.

It is the evil in this world, in one way or the other, which is the true origin from which all my negativity rises. It is evil which allows those normal thoughts to become actual feelings. It is evil which takes my human nature and begs it to lead down the path of resentment and resignation. I will not let the evil in this world defeat me. I will not allow Satan to creep into my thoughts and change my beliefs and allow me to entertain the thought that God has forsaken our officers.

I will be led by my God. I will continue to be a human being who is tired and scared and sad and lonely and nervous and I will continue to want to give up and feel defeated and I will have my moments where I just want to grab my LEO and pull him tight and run with him away from this life, and then I will turn to my God for the strength I need to continue going. I will remind myself that I am not alone. I will remind myself of the others. All the others who feel all the same emotions I do, who all hear the news of a senseless loss of another officer and want to scream as if they just lost a brother.

I will remember that who else has a bond as we do? Who else has such an understanding of the life we live, the fears we face, the heroes which are unrecognized and unappreciated and forgotten so easily? Who else has such a respect for this life and those who lead it and those of us who live to support it? For if not us, who? I will be led by my God and I will remember that he brought me to my LEO to love him because he knew my husband needed a wife like me to love him, to support him when no one else would. To lift him up and encourage him and take pride in his world and make it possible for him to face death and danger and hatred and despair each and every day. I will remember that I too, am called to this life. It is my job, for better or worse, to be the best wife I can be, to honor and love and support my husband, although unlike some other wives, my love and support and devotion and dedication to my husband can actually be the difference that will help him not be defeated, to remain focused, to be able to stay at the top of his game, and despite his brothers and sisters being executed all around him, my love for him, in its totality, may actually be what helps him come home alive, for at least one more day.

The answer is yes. Yes, I am a LEO wife, and NO, I will never be defeated.

I love my LEO.

The Badge

The day was here, they had both waited so long. As she watched her son march down the aisle along with the others in his class, visions of times long past flooded her mind.

Years ago she had been here, as she watched her young husband march down this same aisle. The moment surreal, her emotions, a mix of pride and torture as she knew full well the implications of what the future could possibly hold. She was so proud of her son. He had finally achieved his dream. He was following in his father's footsteps and becoming something bigger than at times he thought he could ever be. She had always held that hope, more of a painful pang actually, that he would find something else to do with his life, but in her heart she somehow knew he would always become a police officer. It was in his blood, it had been such a part of him for so long that she knew he could not resist the calling.

As the ceremony began, memories of earlier years began to rise to the surface. Memories of finding him there, in the closet where his father's uniform hung, sneaking into the forbidden space, off limits for safety reasons, but the urge to understand what kept his father from him beckoned him there. She would find him, studying his father's uniform, memorizing it. His small fingers tracing the outline of the patches she had so lovingly sewn on, tracing his badge as if he were reading braille. He would put his feet into his father's shoes and clomp around the room pretending to be just like his father. A small tear broke free and ran down her cheek as she thought about those times.

She watched as her son and his classmates stood at attention, as they waited for their names to be called to begin the walk across the stage to receive the one thing they all had worked so hard for. That small silver piece of metal, that symbol that meant they were different than ordinary men. That badge. She had a love-hate relationship with that badge. It was so much a part of who she was, what her life was, what her memories were made of, what her character was born from, yet at the same time that badge had taken so much away from the ones who wore it. At times, she had to fight her resentment toward it.

As she watched her son standing there, she struggled to maintain her composure. He was the spitting image of his father. And seeing him there, in that uniform, he didn't just look like his father, he embodied the character of his father, and in a way, she wished he didn't. She wished she could enjoy him growing old without the worry, the fear, the anxiety, the risk. But then again, as she watched him standing there, a sense of pride washed over her. He was just like his father.

He was handsome and strong. He exuded character and strength. She could not believe he was almost twenty five years old, the same age as her husband when he earned his badge. Like father like son she thought as a smile crossed her face, remembering how her husband looked that day so long ago.

It was time. As he heard his name called, he made his way across the stage, he shook the hand of the Chief who advised him to stand and face his mother in the crowd. Confused and off guard, he did as he was instructed to do. An entire auditorium full of family, friends and mentors, he found himself lost for a moment.

As he watched his mother stand and walk to the stage the feelings began to overwhelm him. As she faced him, and her hand unfolded to reveal his father's badge within her grasp, the totality of the moment revealed itself to him. With tears streaming down her face she gently, but precisely, pinned her late husband's badge onto his son, for the first time, but just as she had done countless times in the past. The gravity of the moment coming to reality as he feels his father's presence while the Chief addresses the crowd, offering an inside to the story that was the man, the officer killed in the line of duty so many years before. A man who had never left them, a man who's legacy would now live on through his son.

He learned for the first time that day his father's wish. That his badge be passed on to his son when he took the oath. Even then, all those years before, his father knew. He saw the signs. He felt the blue blood flowing from him to his son and he always knew he would follow in his footsteps. He was only eight years old when they murdered his father. He remembered it as if it were yesterday. He lived his life waiting for the day he would be old enough, man enough to walk in his father's shoes. He knew, just as his father knew, he would grow up one day and be a police officer.

It was who he was born to be. It was who he was taught to be. It was who he was honored to be; a hero, just as his father before him. Today was the day his dream would come true. Just as he stood in the closet all those years ago, his tiny fingers tracing the outline of his father's badge, so it was today, and every day, for as long as he would live to do so.

Forever a LEO Wife

She was restless. It had been one of those days. One of those weeks actually; an officer down on Monday; another on Wednesday; two shot Thursday morning. When would it end? She remembered asking herself that as she read the reports on her laptop. She had told herself a million times before now, this was not the way to pass the time during her husband's shift. But she couldn't sleep anyway. Before she could finish reading, her phone rang. She remembered the urgency in his voice, one of their own had been shot, condition unknown. She immediately looked at the clock. 2:14 a.m. Just 45 minutes from having him home, safe and sound, but she knew better. He would never come home until they caught the bastards who had shot one of their brothers.

She didn't even bother questioning him. She knew him well enough to know his mind was not with her, but with his brothers, his sisters, his department. He would never question his own safety in the fight to find those who had taken one of their own. Frankly, at this point in their relationship, neither would she. She knew not to question his loyalty to the thin blue line. There was no competition.

She never broke through those sacred walls. It was not her place to be. She didn't belong there with him and she didn't take it personally. She had learned years before to find her own niche in his life. A place she could support his calling, a place she could fit in, a place she could make her presence known as a supporter of a life which consistently eliminated her presence.

She learned years ago what her role was, she learned how to play it to her best benefit and she learned to never question feeling left out. She knew it was not of his own doing, it was just a casualty of the job, her emotional wellbeing, that is. She banked on the moment she heard the sound of the garage door, it was the opening of their world together, the place where they had a life of their own, apart from his world…well, in a small way, for a short time. She relished that time. It was her sanctuary with him.

She had never felt love before like she felt for him. She remembered other relationships as a distant quirk in her life, when she remembered them at all. From the moment she met him, she knew it was different. She remembered the early years of their marriage, those tormented years of conflict where they both were still coming to grips with the LEO life; Her expectations being constantly reduced to disappointment, his frustrations of the job being constantly misinterpreted as a lack of sensitivity on his part. She remembered countless nights where she questioned the legitimacy of his lateness, she remembered countless arguments which resulted. She also remembered that the majority of those arguments ended due to him falling asleep while she railed on him for his lack of everything related to her.

She also remembered the night he had his first call to a dead body. She remembered him calling her saying he would be late. She remembered him saying why. She would never forget reading the paper a week later that the body of a nine month old baby girl, who had been sexually assaulted, suffocated and burned to hide the evidence was the call she was so infuriated over. He promised he would be home. He wasn't. She remembered him coming in and heading straight for the shower. She remembered internally accusing him of not being where he claimed to be. She remembered voicing her lack of appreciation for him being four hours late with not so much as a phone call. She remembered giving him the cold shoulder as he collapsed into bed and she rolled away from his touch.

As she saw the news she was angered for a moment at him. Why had he not told her? How was she to know? It was that moment, for the first time in her marriage, she realized what he endured. Her moment of clarity revealed his love for her; what he spared her, what he chose to leave out; what he protected her from, despite his own personal pain. It was at that moment that she realized how selfish she had been, how much pain he held to himself, how much he loved her to spare her the truth of his life. That was the day everything changed. She no longer questioned him.

She became the wife he needed her to be, she gained a new understanding that his love for her surpassed that which he faced on duty and his love for her was so deep that he chose to protect her from the evil which was his life. She began to gain a whole new respect for him and his dedication to his badge, the honor, the pride, the mental anguish he endured, the physical taxing on his body, the emotional toll he internalized in an effort to protect her. She began to realize how deep her love for him was and she began to realize that he had loved her like no other from the beginning.

From that day forward she chose to make the best of her life with him. It was limited; at times she still felt left out. At times she wished he would open up more, she felt she could handle it now. She knew he gave what he could. She understood what he didn't give was to protect himself and to protect her, it wasn't about leaving her out. She learned to make the best of what they had. She focused her attention on her children, on making sure they understood why Daddy was not home, why that was so important, why that had no bearing on his love for them. She brought her children to him as often as she could. She learned to force memories out of moments impossible. She lived her life in charge of the knowledge that every second she had to make a memory was imperative. She lived her life forcing those around her to live as if there may be no tomorrow.

In doing so, she gained a respect from him she would never know the depths of. It was an unspoken understanding. As they grew as a couple, as partners, as parents in a crazy, risk filled love of a life, they grew to understand the unexplainable. They grew to respect the unexpected. They grew to appreciate the moments with unanticipated disappointments. They grew to appreciate each moment for what it was, and not what they thought they wanted it to be. They grew in love. And she knew it. She felt it. She lived it. She loved it. She relished it while in the depths of her soul, she always feared it still.

The sound of the alarm shook her. It had happened just the same so many times before. Her last thought before escaping to sleep was reading the news, waiting for him to return, listening for the garage door which never seemed to come. The alarm, the sounding of reality that today was yet another day she would have to face. Yet another day she awoke alone, looked over to his side of the bed to find her hand still reaching for him, wishing for a different shift, wishing he were there to help her get her children up out of bed and off to school. This was her life though, she was prepared for it years in advance. She had awoken from this dream for several years now, although each day she assumed would be the day she would awaken to a different reality. How long did you have to be a LEO wife before you became accustomed to it? She still found herself asking the same question. She begged it to just be a dream…but it was real.

As she pulled herself out of bed, again…she prepared herself for another day; another day as a LEO wife, another day doing most things by herself, another day explaining to her children that Daddy loved them, he wanted to be there with them, he just had such an important job that he could not be there with them now.

As she stood and walked to her bathroom to shower, she stopped where she did each day. She stopped at his picture beside her bed, the picture which sat above the box which held the flag from his funeral. She kissed him. She asked for his help. She told him how much she loved him and missed him. She asked him to be with her through another day raising their children alone. She asked him to be with her and never leave her dreams, her memories, her thoughts.

She once again asked for another day with him by her side, even if only in her dreams.

An Officer's POV

An Officer's Will

He sat against his cruiser as a light snow fell around him, the pulses from his strobes making the soft snow flakes appear to dance in the darkness. He tried to remember how he got there, on the ground beside his car. His body felt like he had been run over by a truck. His chest burned under his vest. His arms and legs were on fire and he couldn't figure out why. Images of his wife kept flashing through his mind, he imagined her looking down at him, begging him to hold on, to not give up, to come home to her. The coldness of the snow around him reminded him to pay attention, to stay awake. Everything was so hazy, he struggled to meticulously recall the incident, as he was trained to do. He remembered pulling a car over out here on this remote stretch of highway. He remembered walking up to the driver's window and politely asking for license, registration and insurance cards. However, he could not remember how he got to where he now lay. His body hurting, he feels himself physically tiring. Like an alarm of sorts, again he hears his wife's voice, leading him, instructing him, forcing his focus. He tells her he loves her.

The night, completely silent except the sound of his own breath hitting bitter cold air, the sound of dispatch calling his unit number interrupts his drifting. He tries to answer on his portable but he can't find it. He doesn't understand. It's always on his belt. He listens to the emergency tones and he continues to hear dispatch reporting, "Officer down", while units start marking up, panic in their voices.

A sense of urgency hits him at the same time. Instinctively thinking he should go help the officer in trouble he tries to stand but his legs refuse to answer the command. His weakness and drifting now being replaced with anger, he is getting pissed off. "Why won't my body do what I tell it to? What is wrong with me?" He does not understand and he cannot remember. A twinge of fear begins to creep over him but mostly he is just mad at himself. He thinks maybe he got caught up in the routine, maybe he got complacent thinking nothing bad could happen to him, he was well trained and in great shape. He had been doing this for years.

The sound of sirens in the distance caught his attention, and he looked around and saw the pulsing strobes of lights headed towards him. He watched as they grew closer and the sirens got louder and louder. He didn't remember calling for backup…why were there so many of them? The entire road was covered with lights and the sounds of sirens and screaming engines growing louder and louder.

The sound of snow cracking as tires screech to a halt, he can hear doors open and the familiar sound of boots hitting pavement in rapid movement. He hears familiar voices crying his name but he is too tired to answer now. He senses familiar smells and hears the voice of his partner, his best friend telling him it's going to be alright; telling him to hang in there, telling him to fight, telling him, "Do not give up, do not let go. Fight dammit, you fight."

He can't tell them what happened but his dash camera will tell his story for him. It shows him stopping the car and walking up to the driver and asking for the information. It records the driver's angry voice saying, "&%#^% you Pig!" It then records the sound of gunshots, the flashes of light from the muzzle lighting up the night. It records him stumbling backwards as he draws his weapon. It records his own shots striking the car and the windows shattering from the impact of bullets. It records him backing away and firing as he tries to find cover. It records the suspect exiting his car, shooting at the officer.

It records the sound of bullets striking the officers vest and others as they tear into his body. It records his cries of pain as he is struck and the determination in his voice as he continues to fire back, still functioning as an officer, shouting commands at the suspect to drop his weapon. It records the suspect's gun being knocked from his grasp by a bullet and the impact of other bullets as they meet the suspect's body. It records the beastly scream the suspect gives as he then charges the officer empty handed. It records the sound of bodies crashing together and falling onto the ground. It records screams and fists impacting on flesh. It then records one more shot fired, followed by silence. It records the sound of heavy breathing and moaning and the sound of handcuffs snapping around wrists. It records the sound of an officer trying to sit up and yelling at his body to do what he wants. It records him telling his wife he loves her and to stop worrying. It records his car radio asking for his status. It records the sounds of emergency tones and the call for an officer down. It records the response from his brothers and the panic in their voices. It records the sound of their sirens getting closer and the sound of them arriving. It records the sound of their voices giving him encouragement and help and asking him to hold on.

What it does not record is the future. It does not record the trauma he has received both mentally and physically. It does not record the trampled and blood soaked snow that surrounds him, other cameras will record that scene. It does not record the scars he has received and will carry with him for the rest of his life. It does not record the nightmares that haunt him each time he closes his eyes. It does not record the struggles he will face over the next years. It does not record the sacrifices he has to make or the changes that night forced upon him. No longer does he patrol the highways he loved. No longer does he work with his friends and partners. No longer does he carry the badge that he loves so much. His injuries would not allow him to return to the job he loves still to this day. He still stands upon the thin blue line though. Now he is a role model, a teacher, an example to others who wish to stand the line also. He shows his video and he teaches others about the dangers. He teaches others about the will to survive, the will to overcome against all odds. He shows them the importance of never giving up and continuing to fight, regardless of the circumstance. He shows them that having the will to win is as important as having the skills to win. He is an example of the good warrior, the warrior with a human spirit, the warrior with a soul.

He is and always will be a HERO. He is a police officer.

A Mother's Love

Without Limits

Regardless of what you are told; regardless of your expectations; nothing can prepare you for that moment. It is a power so overwhelming, so engulfing, so far beyond any capacity which you ever knew existed. It is the power of love; yet it is love like none you have ever experienced before, and it is a love which cannot be substituted by or duplicated for another. It is pure, unique, unequivocal and completely encompassing love. It is a mother's love for her child. I say child and not children because it is a love completely individual and unique for each child a mother brings into this world. In that moment…that long anticipated moment when a mother first hears her child's voice, followed by the very first sight of her child's eyes, the touch of her child's skin on her skin, life forever changes in an instant. Although already fully in love with her child, bonded with her child, familiar with her child's routine and personality from within the womb, the moment God breathes life into a child in the outside world beyond the womb, it instantly becomes a love which surpasses any emotional attachments previously understood.

"A mother's love for her child is like nothing else in the world. It knows no law, no pity, it dares all things and crushes down remorselessly all that stands in its path." -Agatha Christie

She anxiously watched them through the kitchen window. One eye on the clock, one eye on her boys, the eyes in the back of her head as well as her ears always focused on the sound of the garage door. She struggled to keep her inner panic under control. She had been here before, although this time was different. She had a nauseas pit in her stomach, and a knot in her throat, a gut feeling and a sixth sense that something was different. For whatever reason, she knew, and she would spend the next two hours hoping against hope that she was wrong.

Emotions and visions becoming entangled in her thoughts, she found herself trying to shake the images from her mind, like an etch-a-sketch being shaken clean of all mistakes. She played the last moments over and over again in her mind, finding herself creating different endings...any ending other than what she felt was true. Startled by the voice coming from her waist, "Mommy where's Daddy?" She had been so lost in her fears she completely missed her boys coming back inside the house. "Daddy had to work late. He's taking care of something very important, so it might be a while before we see him." She ushered them off to get cleaned up for lunch, and she knew by the clock and the nausea and the knot in her throat it was time to call her mother. As she picked up the phone she looked at the numbers which now looked completely foreign. It took her almost ten minutes to remember a number she had known by heart for over twenty years.

The doorbell sounded different in her mind than it did when it finally sounded. In her visions it was almost in slow motion, loud with vibrato which lingered in the air. Now, to hear it echoing down the front entry hall she was ironically reminded of her life without the availability of her husband. As the doorbell chimed an awful chime, short lived and flat, followed by a clear buzz of an electrical short, she was reminded of yet another project which had not been checked off the list. Not wanting her children to hear or witness what might happen next, but before she could even speak, her mother was already headed to the stairs. The statement she made seemed so matter of fact, "Not inside this house. You go out on the porch and close the door behind you."

It seemed so callus to be the last thing her own mother said as she went to get the news that could change her forever, but her own instinct as a mother completely understood what eternal damage her boys would suffer should the sound of their mother's cries of agony be embedded in their minds. She waited until her mother topped the stairs and quietly opened the door.

Two men, two words; The Chief spoke while her husband's partner stood prepared to physically catch her. Two words, "He's alive." She didn't need to hear the rest. She didn't want to hear it. She wanted to keep those two words, just those two words, but she saw the tears welling in the eyes of her husband's partner. They were like brothers, two partners, together for eight years now, sworn to protect each other no matter what. She felt the knot welling up again, she could see the truth in his eyes, she had felt it all day. "Don't say it....don't you dare say it! I just want those two words! I JUST WANT THOSE TWO WORDS!"

She crumpled into his arms and no sooner than she felt her own tears begin to roll down her cheeks, she felt the warmth of the tears of his partner as they began to fall, absorbing into her hair. "I just want those two words," she softly whimpered now, resigned to the knowledge that there was so much more to come. As they composed themselves the Chief advised, "You need to have your mother come with you and the boys to the hospital now, in case you have to say goodbye."

She slowly climbed the stairs, in her mind a million conversations passed to her from her mother, so many she had really not taken too seriously, now all flowing like raging flood waters into the forethought of her conscience. "If you have children with an officer you must be prepared to do it alone." "You never know if you will have a husband when you wake up in the morning but you cannot live in fear of that, you accept it and live your life, just like I did with you girls and your father." "If you expect this marriage to work you best lose your selfishness young lady and tend to those boys while you talk roses about their father, you knew this going in and it's not his fault some man robbed a liquor store tonight."

On, and on and on they flowed, now coming like a whirlwind of advice and lectures all rolled together as she searched her memory for the story of how to tell her children something bad had happened. As she opened the bedroom door the memory hit her like a wave; one she had allowed to wash back out with the tide so many years before. As she saw her mother sitting on the edge of the bed with her grandchildren, the memory of her and her sister rushed back to her, sitting on the bed with the yellow comforter, the one with the little white embroidered daisies, as their mother explained that their father wasn't coming home.

In that second she realized she had already announced it to her own boys earlier in the day, just as her mother did so many years before. "Your father is doing something very important...he's in heaven now with Jesus. He's watching over all of Daddy's officer friends, and us too. It might be a while before we see him, but one day we will see him again."

A peace enveloped her like a blanket. The pit in her stomach was gone. The knot in her throat had vanished. She had no idea of knowing earlier when she spoke those words that God was giving her the answer. As she walked into the room and sat on the bed she calmly spoke to her children in a way only a mother can, "Remember I told you earlier your father had to work late and he was doing something very important and it might be a while before you would see him? Well, Daddy was watching over his other officer's today and he got hurt, he got hurt real bad, but he's going to be alright and we're going to go see him now, but it might be a while before he gets to come home."

She looked into the eyes of her own mother, a look of surprise mixed with confusion on her face, clearly asking without speaking why she would give her children that hope after the cries she had just heard coming from the porch while standing at the top of the stairs. "How do you know Daddy's going to be alright Mommy?" "Because son, God told me earlier today. I just didn't understand until now."

It was Mother's Day, four months later, she stood in the kitchen with her mother, peeling potatoes,

147

looking out the back window at her husband playing with his son's. "How did you know that day he was going to make it?" her mother asked. "Call it a gut feeling I guess. I said almost the same thing to the boys earlier in the day that you did when you told us Dad died, but it came out different. I left off a few words. When I remembered that, I just knew. I guess sometimes mothers just know."

She was thankful that Mother's Day for the truths her mother always told. She was prepared to handle life as an officer's wife and she was well prepared to be the mother of an officer's children. There certainly was no doubt, she knew how to listen to God now as well.

An Officer's POV

Monster in the Night

He needed her. He needed her like he had never needed her before. He had just finished what was probably the worst call of his career. Other officers referred to them as the "bad ones." The calls that you can't describe any other way except that it was a bad one. It was not dispatched that way. A simple check welfare call. Simple, he thought as he made his way there. No need to rush to it. He was about to be proved wrong, although he had no way of knowing that. He did not know that his world was about to change, that he was about to change. He did not know that he was about to meet evil face to face and it would drastically and forever change him. He checks out at the address and particulars, a mother can't get in touch with her daughter. Probably has had the phone shut off he thought to himself, not the best neighborhood, but not the worst either.

Upon arrival, he goes to the door and listens as a light rain starts to fall. Hearing nothing, he knocks on the door, no response. He sees a car in the driveway. No lights on inside. He has dispatch check the call history and while he waits, he decides to walk around the house. As he heads for the back door, he peers into the windows. Nothing out of the ordinary, maybe she's at a friends or something.

As he rounds the corner of the house, he freezes. Something alerts him that something is not right. The back door is slightly open. He draws his weapon and pushes the door open, the beam of his flashlight piercing the darkness. Slowly he enters the kitchen and the smell of fresh blood rushes his senses. He quietly radios for assistance, knowing it will take a while and knowing it is up to him to keep checking. He proceeds around the corner, just then his flashlight meets and illuminates the crumpled form of a young girl laying in the hallway, a pool of blood surrounding her. He checks her, but she is gone, two jagged holes in her back tell him that a gun was used. His senses on high alert he proceeds further into the house. Nothing, no signs of a struggle, no signs of anything out of the ordinary except her lifeless body.

He begins to climb the stairs, slowly, cautiously, his weapon at the ready. He gets to a bedroom, slowly opens the door, trying to be quiet. The beam of his flashlight reveals a child's room, a crib, toys on the floor. He whispers a silent prayer hoping against hope. He reaches the crib and sees a small form under a blanket. His hand trembles as he reaches out and pulls the blanket back.

A tear breaks free and runs down his cheek and a part of his soul dies. Why the baby? God, why to a child? What did he do to deserve this? He finds his radio and pushes the emergency button hoping that other officers will get there faster although he can't know, his radio turned down as to not give him away. Everything in him wants to scream into it for them to hurry but he can't. He has to do this alone. He strains to hear the sound of a siren in the distance but there is only the sound of his heart beating out of his vest. He prepares to finish checking the rest of the rooms when a sound catches his ear; he makes his way to the door and listens. He hears moaning from inside the room. He pushes the door open, ready to defend himself, but there is no need. His light outlines the form of a man, slumped against the bed and the wall, blood covering his chest, and dripping from his lips. A gun lays at his side. He kicks the gun away as the monster looks up at him, his eyes pleading for help.

He stares at him, his gun in his hand, and a feeling so strong begins to rise up in him. He could end this, he could give them justice but he knows he can't. There would be no way to explain his actions. The mans eyes plead with him for help, his arms shaking as he musters the strength to reach out for help, but the monster is denied. His rage overpowering, he simply stands over him and watches, almost delighted, as death creeps across the monsters face and claims him. He smiles and knows it was the last vision he saw as he drifted off to hell.

Suddenly the rage is replaced by guilt. Why did he not get to the call sooner? Why did he assume that it would turn out alright? These calls always turned out alright. If he had driven just a little faster, moved a little quicker, maybe he could have stopped him. Why? His thoughts interrupted as he begins to hear sirens in the background getting closer, he grabs his radio and tells them to slow down, he is not in danger and there is no point in rushing.

The next several hours were a blur, interviews with detectives, paperwork, reports, the same story told over and over, they were already gone when he got there. He did not think that anyone would care if he told them he just watched as the suspect bled to death in front of him, he could not tell that part, at least not now. He was sure that he did what he had to do. He knew he couldn't save the monster even if he had tried to, he was too far gone. He knew without a doubt there was a young mother and her baby who were glad he did not help their killer, that he let him suffer his last few moments, at least that's how he wanted to remember it. He also knew that he would carry that with him forever. That for the first time in his career he had gone against his oath to protect life. He knew that it could never be undone and he hoped that when his time came, God would understand and forgive him.

He walked outside into the early morning darkness and let the rain fall on him. He tried to let the rain wash away the remnants of the evil he had faced. He wished the rain would wash away his thoughts and memories but knew that it could never be erased. He knew they would always be with him now. Slowly he made his way to his car and started the drive home, slowly he made his way towards his house, his wife, his family. He needed them. He needed to see their faces, to hear their voices, to feel their touch. As he drove, he realized just how much lately he had been neglecting them, working a lot of extra details, missing special occasions for a little extra money each pay day. His wife used to complain about him working so much, about him being gone and putting the job first, but the last couple of years she had started just doing things by herself and taking care of what needed to be done. He was proud of her for that, she had matured well past her young age. He wished he had told her that more often.

He pulled into the garage and quietly went inside. He stopped at his son's room and watched him sleeping for a moment. Thanking God for giving him another chance. He showered quietly and as he climbs into bed beside his wife, instinctively in her sleep she reaches out to touch him, her hand on his chest. It is what he needs and he begins to cry softly in the darkness. She wakens yet says nothing knowing he will talk when he can. She holds him and tells him it will be alright, that she loves him and she is there for him as his exhaustion allows him to fade into sleep. Sleep forever filled with monsters.

What is a Police Wife?

by Sgt. Phil Giffen; a tribute to the love of his life, his Police Wife, Gina

A tribute from a grateful officer/husband.

A police wife is more courageous than her police officer. He has a gun, a vest and other officers. She faces these things alone with just her love to get her through it. She uses the strength of her character to survive.

She knows when he has had a bad day.

She understands when he says, "I cant." She waits until he can.

She knows when to ask and when to just reach out and touch his arm. She is always there for him.

She never lets him leave without a kiss and an I love you. Even when she is mad at him.

She means it with all her heart and soul when she says, "I love you and be careful."

She puts a blue candle in her window to remember the fallen.

She has learned to accept what she cannot change.

She accepts that strangers will always come first when he is working. She won't like it though.

She has learned to be flexible.

She has found strength she did not know she had.

She has found courage she did not know existed.

She has known sorrow and pain, mind numbing, heart stopping sorrow and pain and yet she made it through and found peace.

She knows the joy of a simple note left on the counter after he left for work.

She knows the happiness that five minutes stolen in a parking lot brings.

She stands tall in the face of adversity.

She holds her head high when people mock him or make disparaging comments about his profession.

She comforts him when he is hurting.

She encourages him when he is down.

She gives him strength when he is weak.

She holds him when words wont help.

She calms him in the darkness when the demons wont let him rest.

She leads him from the darkness of the evil he works in at the end of his shift.

She waits patiently for his return at the end of his shift.

My police wife, as I like to say is crunchy on the outside, but tender on the inside.

She is crunchy to protect herself from the looks and words of others.

She is crunchy to help her make it through her days and nights spent alone.

She is crunchy to protect his family while he protects others.

She only shows her tenderness to those that understand her life.

She cries when he leaves to face the unknown.

She cries when she is alone in bed.

She prays as she watches him drive away.

She lays awake, waiting for him when she should be sleeping.

She longs for the sound of his keys in the door, the sound of velcro and belt keepers.

Her heart skips a beat when the phone rings at night and he is not there.

She pauses when she hears a siren, hoping he is being careful.

She understands what no one else can.

She cherishes each and every moment she has with him.

She loves him when others hate him and what he stands for.

She goes with him to comfort others who have paid the ultimate sacrifice, hoping it is never her.

My wife is a police wife and she knows all these things. She is my best friend, my support and MY HERO. I love her so much and she makes me so proud.

This is My Camelot

Her heart skipped a beat when she heard the doorbell ring, although not out of surprise, she had the UPS tracking screen up on her computer for the past three days. As she hurried into the kitchen with the box she found herself reaching for a butter knife as the first reachable object in which to assist her. Her pride beaming as she removed the photos from the packaging. Her wedding photos; and they were just as perfect as she expected them to be. Her with him, in his brand new uniform, so in love, so perfect. That whole day was so perfect. As hectic as it had been

161

planning a wedding while her fiance was finishing up with Police Academy, still she had no regrets. It was all done now. Academy, the wedding, moving into the small but perfect house they were going to fix up together. Looking at those pictures seemed somehow to give her the authentication of her life. She was officially a police wife, and it had been such a long journey. As she dialed his number with great anticipation of sharing the good news - no answer. He must be on a call. She dialed her mother instead.

She spent the better part of the day dividing up the photos; those for his family, these for hers. She had been purchasing frames for months, everyone laughing at her as she always seemed to pick up a new frame regardless of where she was on any given day. She knew she would need them though, and today proved the smartness of her fore-thinking. She had plenty of frames in all the right sizes to begin to adorn the small little house with the memory of that perfect day.

She spent hours unpacking boxes, even got the curtains hung in the living room. She couldn't wait for his shift to end. He would be so thrilled to see all the work she had put into that afternoon. She decided to make his favorite dinner as well. The past two weeks since the wedding and graduation had been so hectic, she was looking forward to an evening where they could just decompress and enjoy their new life together, even if dinner had to be at 11:00 p.m. Wondering about dessert she gave him a quick call - no answer. That twinge of anxiety mixed with annoyance entered her mind. She quickly dismissed it. After all, this is what being a police wife is all about.

An hour had passed since he was due home, thirty minutes had passed since he text her saying he would be home in ten minutes. As she checked on the food she was trying to keep warm without drying out completely, she caught herself slamming the oven door. As she looked out the front windows there was no sign of him. As usual.

The sound of his keys hitting the counter woke her. She must have dozed off on the couch. She squinted as she took a second look at the clock...is that right? 2:40 a.m.?

"What took so long?" she asked in as loving of a voice as she could muster.

"I'm sorry Babe, I had a drunk get physical with me then I was finally done with that, and some asshole drove his semi right into the guardrail. Took us three hours to clear. I'm beat, I gotta take a shower, I smell like death and I gotta be back on at 0700 to cover for Jimmy."

0700? Now she was past being irritated. "Could you speak in English time, please, what time do you have to be back? You're not supposed to be back until 3:00 p.m. tomorrow afternoon?"

"0700, as in 7:00 a.m.! Jimmy's taking a personal day and I offered to cover for him. Now, I'm getting in the shower."

She was fuming. "Alright, first of all, you could have called to let me know you would be so late, I made dinner and you text me saying you were ten minutes away. And not that you would even notice but I've worked my ass off today trying to get this house put together and make a nice meal for you and we got our wedding pictures in and I was really excited to show you!"

He interrupted her and calmly said, "I'm sorry you're upset. I'm covered in blood that's not mine, and oil and mud and honestly food is the last thing on my mind and I'm going to take a shower and go to bed. I can look at some pictures that cost way too much anyway tomorrow."

Now furious, she screamed at him, "YOU WON'T BE HERE TOMORROW, REMEMBER?! You'll be there for your friend Jimmy, just not for your wife!"

He grabbed a beer and as he headed down the hall he passed a wall of framed wedding photos. "Good thing I offered to cover for him, someones got to pay for these damn pictures."

And so it began. Her perfect life as a police wife. Over the next few years they continued to have their moments. The surprise birthday party she planned for him: house full of family and what few friends they had left; he never showed up. The weekend getaway she had planned for months, canceled at the last minute. Her first ultrasound. Their first Thanksgiving in the new little house.

She honestly couldn't remember when it all stopped bothering her. There were times it still did, but she had long since accepted that this was how it would be. And things in her world were changing. Any thoughts of selfishness had been replaced with a genuine fear. The world seemed to be forgetting who her husband was. There seemed to be no respect for him or his duty or service. She found herself growing from a young and somewhat self-centered wife to a rapidly matured woman and an independent mother. She was indeed a completely different girl than she was just five years before and she longed for simpler days when a cold dinner or a late shift were all she had to complain about.

Perhaps she softened to his needs that first time he came home after pulling a dead baby from the wreckage. Or perhaps it was the time he witnessed the terror in the eyes of a rape victim he was trying to help. Even she had to find a way to dull her senses when the stench of his uniform let her know before he did that his last call of the day was to a dead body. It didn't seem odd to her that she simply ran a hot load of bleach water through the washer after she cleaned his uniforms. It never occurred to her that this was her way of not only killing germs, but cleansing memories.

More than those normal oddities, she felt it was something more. Some stronger pull that had her gravitating towards understanding and compassion and patience and pride for what he endured. For the first time in five years, she felt his fear. It was unspeakable. It was taboo. The thought of her law enforcement officer even eluding to being fearful in his duty was foreign to her. But she sensed it. She had been feeling it for months. They both watched the numbers rise as the thin blue line began to fall. It was ceremonial loss. Formal death.

As another story hit the press she watched as he adorned his black badge band, once again. She watched as departments released their statements and spoke of yet another hero fallen. Another family left in mourning. Another father taken from his children. They watched the funeral processions as they also watched the lack of public interest. She watched him age quickly. She noticed him checking his clips and taser and gear more meticulously than ever before. She watched him linger before getting into his uniform. She watched him begin to change into something he was never allowed to be while in that uniform. She watched her LEO longing to be a husband; and five years before, that young princess bride longed for him to be just that. She knew she had to make sure he was just the opposite. Now, she had to be strong enough, selfless enough and police wife enough to make sure he was a LEO first and her husband second.

One thing she had learned without a doubt, in order for her husband to come home, he had to be the best officer he could be on duty. Without a second thought she became his biggest cheerleader. She went out of her way to encourage him and assure him that she and his children were just fine. She lived life the way he needed her to in order for his focus to be on protecting himself and others. She put her personal needs aside as she watched the man she loved struggle with his own human emotion. She became the strength he needed her to be and they were both better for it.

Yes, something changed in her. Perhaps she just matured as she learned about the LEO life. Perhaps it was only through those early arguments she evolved into who she was today. Perhaps she too had to become seasoned in the ways of law enforcement to be able to understand what is really important. One thing she knows for sure....her husband is her hero because he is a LEO and there certainly is no doubt, this is her Camelot.

CPSIA information can be obtained
at www.ICGtesting.com
Printed in the USA
BVHW08s0222130818
524249BV00002B/96/P